BEARS

RULERS OF THE WILDERNESS

Robert Elman

LONGMEADOW
PRESS

This 1992 edition published by Longmeadow Press,
201 High Ridge Road, Stamford, CT 06904.

This book was designed and produced by
Todtri Productions Limited
P.O. Box 20058
New York, NY 10023-1482

Printed and Bound in Singapore

Library of Congress Catalog Number 92-52697
ISBN 0-681-41589-4

Printed and Bound in Singapore

0 9 8 7 6 5 4 3 2 1

Author: Robert Elman

Producer: Robert M. Tod
Designer and Art Director: Mark Weinberg
Editor: Mary Forsell
Typeset and Page Makeup: Strong Silent Type/NYC

TABLE OF CONTENTS

INTRODUCTION
AN OVERVIEW

Throughout history, man has been amused, mystified, fascinated, and often terrified by bears. Several species of bears rank as the world's largest animals in the order Carnivora, and yet all but one—the exceptionally predatory polar bear, which lives where vegetation is absent or scant—are the least carnivorous of carnivores. The behavior of most species is paradoxical in other ways as well. They tend to be timid with regard to the unfamiliar and especially in their avoidance of human beings, yet their ferocity is legendary. Except when courting and mating or when a female is rearing its young, they are solitary creatures, intolerant of intrusion by their own kind, but sometimes they congregate in considerable numbers, and for the most part peacefully, to gorge themselves where food becomes abnormally plentiful. To a human observer, their behavior occasionally seems pointless or dim-witted, but instances revealing astonishing intelligence are far more numerous. They walk with a lumbering, awkward-looking, rolling gait, but they can also gallop and, indeed, move with incredible speed.

In many parts of Europe and particularly in Russia, brown bears have traditionally been utilized as circus performers, trained to balance and circle about on a small drum, ride a tricycle, pull a cart, even wrestle playfully and harmlessly with the trainer. Although the animal is generally muzzled and sometimes leashed or chained, it remains capable of inflicting terrible injury with its claws, powerful limbs, and sheer weight. Undoubtedly, many a trainer has had moments of severe anxiety when a suddenly recalcitrant performer refused to loosen its bear hug. Still, the Eurasian brown bear is easily trained when young, and this seems all the more incredible since taxonomists now agree that it is the very same species as North America's grizzly, perhaps the most ferocious of all bears. And in Europe, for that matter, its behavior in the wild has inspired tales of terror.

A similar case is that of India's famous dancing bears, trained to perform by itinerant entertainers. Most of these animals are of sloth bear (also known as Indian bear) ori-

gin. This is considered to be one of the most dangerous animals of the jungles of India and Ceylon. In Ceylonese villages, only a rogue elephant is said to arouse more fear. Of course, the elephant is another paradoxical creature, an animal that is sometimes murderous in the wild but almost appears to have a sense of humor and certainly shows affection when entertaining a circus audience.

Although I have never sought intimate contact with bears in the wild—observation from a distance having seemed more sensible and sufficiently fulfilling—I have had several encounters. The first occurred half a century ago, when I was about ten. It amused me then and the memory still does, but I would have been panicked had I known how narrowly tragedy was averted. My family was driving from lower Wyoming up to Montana, and we decided to detour slightly for a tour of Yellowstone Park. Even in those days, park rangers labored valiantly to safeguard visitors from their own folly, and signs were posted to warn—in fact, command—tourists not to feed or even approach the bears.

Few visitors paid the slightest attention to those signs, and grizzlies prowled the roadsides like city panhandlers, begging alms in the form of food from the motorists who stopped to photograph and gaze at them, enraptured by their size; their obvious power; their sometimes comic antics; seemingly anthropomorphic poses, gestures, and actions; and their deceptive appearance of gentleness.

My father was in the driver's seat, my mother next to him, and I was in back when we stopped on the shoulder of the road to join a couple of other carloads in watching three grizzlies amble back and forth along the opposite shoulder, begging. Each of them shuffled along for several yards, then turned abruptly and shuffled back, rather like caged lions eyeing their observers. Several tidbits—the remains of half-eaten sandwiches, I think—were tossed from the first car in line, and two of the rotund shufflers pounced on the morsels with a startling, leonine agility. The third, by far the largest of the trio, was a very thickly furred brown behemoth that moved with slow deliberation out onto the road, blocking traffic.

It was my father's habit to keep paper bags of fruits and sweets on the front seat between him and my mother. On this warm day the car windows were open, and Dad tossed out a plum. As it bounced twice and rolled along the road, the big grizzly followed it, head low and sniffing, and gulped it down. I had in hand a little Kodak box camera. I started to get out of the car, intent on snapping close-up pictures that would be the envy of every kid in school.

"Get in here," Dad ordered. "Shut that door and roll up your window." Fortunately for me, although I lacked the sense or experience to fear the grizzly, I had quite enough experience to fear the consequences of defying Dad's orders.

What finally scared me was the realization that the car was rocking slightly from side to side, then rocking more severely. With one paw that bear, probably weighing between four hundred and five hundred pounds (the estimated weight of inland grizzlies is another common exaggeration), was heaving and swaying our heavy four-door sedan. Momentarily its left forepaw dangled limply, then rose, reached through the window, and as slowly, as halfheartedly as a circus bear, swiped at my father's face without quite touching it, and drew back to rest—lightly—on the lower edge of the driver's window. With an alacrity I had never seen in him before, Dad cranked the window up.

A DISPUTED CLAIM.-

5

In evolutionary terms relating to long-extinct mammals of the family Miacidae, bears can be said to be related (albeit distantly) both to raccoons and dogs. They appear to have comparable—that is, wondrous—intelligence, and, like raccoons and dogs, they are strongly attracted to the most easily obtained food, even where such feeding is likely to bring contact and conflict with humans. Just as garbage dumps mean easy pickings, so do individual trash cans next to homes. Some years ago I had a cabin in a thickly populated resort area of the Pocono Mountains in Pennsylvania (a state notable for its excellent wildlife management and consequently large black bear population). Bears tend to be nocturnal or at least crepuscular where conflict with humans is frequent, but in this vicinity they sometimes raided backyards in broad daylight.

One morning I glanced out the window and saw a large black bear—perhaps three hundred pounds or more—wrestling the lid off the garbage can behind my kitchen. Glistening black and autumn-fat, this animal had a cocoa-brown snout and an irregular white chest blaze.

I could not be certain, but I thought I recognized it as a sow bear I had previously seen nearby in the woods, accompanied by a single cub. Although no cub was in sight now, my suspicion that it was the same bear reinforced my instant decision to confine my observation to watching through the window. Black bears are normally not aggressive, but they have been known to kill. All mother bears are fiercely protective of their young, and good judgment dictates no interference or close approach.

The bear found nothing worthwhile in my trash and soon turned back to the dirt road and proceeded to the next cabin, perhaps a hundred yards away. Walking with slow, heavy undulations that made its glossy coat ripple, the sow bear went directly to another trash can and knocked it over with a quick, deft sideswipe of its left paw. A metal can, it came down on gravel with a reverberating clang, at which the bear flinched and jumped back, but immediately advanced again to nose amid its contents. The cabin's owner, a year-round resident, was a portly, sweet-tempered woman in her seventies.

As the bear pawed about investigating trash-can scraps, the woman emerged from the cabin door on the run, straw broom in hand, shouting, "Scat, damn it! Get out of here!"

Some animals are, by the nature of their facial bone structure and musculature, expressionless, but dogs, raccoons, and bears can convey a great deal through facial expression as well as action. I was now watching with binoculars, and observed that bear looked utterly amazed. The animal hunched back, seeming to cringe, but stood its ground as the woman advanced, broom raised high. At the last instant, as the broom came down, the bear raised its front feet a few inches off the ground and swung around in retreat on its hind feet, spinning like a toy on a stick. The broom came down heavily on its rump as it galloped away, across the road and into the woods.

I still believe it was the mother bear of my previous sighting, but if the cub had been nearby the mother bear might well have mauled or killed its attacker instead of retreating. The behavior of bears during a confrontation is almost always unpredictable, but to challenge one—especially a mother bear—is a fool's gamble. My elderly neighbor, having lived in bear country for many years, surely knew that and evidently did not care. In some people, familiarity breeds foolhardiness, which all too often leads to tragedy. Surely that woman was blessed with good fortune.

She went back into her cabin and phoned the local game protector (as game wardens are called in Pennsylvania). He came quickly, with a tranquilizer gun, an assistant, and a truck on which were mounted a hoist and a cagelike compartment, intending to drug the bear and relocate it somewhere back in the mountains. If my recollection is correct, he also had a hound with him. He hunted hard, found tracks, scat, and other signs, but neither he nor anyone ever saw that bear again. In addition to being unpredictable, bears that have had experience with humans can sometimes be very cunning at eluding pursuit.

Physical Characteristics of Bears

People think of bears as large animals and, in general, so they are. Among the various species, however, size varies considerably. Most species weigh between two hundred and four hundred pounds at maturity, assuming they live in good habitat. A mature sun bear, smallest of the lot, may weigh as much as two hundred pounds, but is much more likely to scale half of that, sometimes less. A mature polar bear generally weighs about one thousand pounds—half a ton, give or take a couple of hundred pounds—and the largest specimen ever recorded was a male reported to weigh 2,210 pounds! A mature Alaskan brown bear (a subspecies of grizzly and therefore the same species as the various European and Asian brown bears) is very nearly as large as the polar bear, and specimens as heavy as seventeen hundred and even eighteen hundred pounds have been reported. The closely related subspecies of the Kamchatka Peninsula, which juts southward from Siberian Russia between the Sea of Okhotsk and the Bering Sea, is even larger. Actually, at least two subspecies exist on the peninsula, one of them no larger than a European brown bear. The giant variety, however, is a black-colored brown reported to weigh as much as eighteen hundred pounds.

Native legends tell of giant specimens weighing more than twenty-five hundred pounds. Because of the wildness, remoteness, harsh climate, and dense scrub vegetation of the region, neither hunters nor scientists have found such specimens in modern times, but there is evidence that they exist. A researcher from the State Museum of Natural History at Stockholm spent two years there, and among his discoveries were incredible tracks in the snow. Moreover, he was shown a gigantic bear skull and skin whose measurements confirmed the legends of beasts weighing perhaps a ton. Undoubtedly, these supremely elusive creatures are the world's largest bears.

Although various species exhibit pronounced physical differences, and each is unique in several ways or many, a number of valid generalizations can be made. Bears are heavily built creatures, with thick, somewhat ponderous bodies; short, strong legs; a tail so short that it is often hidden in the fur; a short, thick neck; a large, rounded head with a somewhat pointed muzzle; short ears; and small eyes. The frontward-oriented eyes, among other characteristics, mark them as basically carnivorous. This binocular vision has evolved in predators to aid in sighting, stalking, or chasing prey and making accurate lunges, whereas the sideward-oriented eyes of herbivores, set differently in the skull, give them a wider arc of sideward and even rearward vision to help in detecting and escaping from approaching predators.

Their omnivorous rather than truly carnivorous habits are also manifest in their physiology. The dental formation is the same as in dogs and wolves, with forty-two teeth, but the postcarnassials have evolved into flat, crushing teeth rather than the cutting teeth of other carnivores, and the tuberculoid shape of the molar crowns also indicates an omnivorous diet.

The paws each have five toes, nonretractile claws, and naked soles—except in the case of the polar bear, which has developed hairy soles for insulation and to aid in walking over icy and snow-blanketed surfaces. Like humans, bears have a plantigrade walk, the entire sole of the foot contacting the ground with each step, an unusual trait in mammals. This is what gives them their ponderous gait—a dangerously deceptive characteristic. When appropriately motivated, they can leap surprisingly long distances with ease and grace, and can run with astonishing speed. If a bear charges a person from a distance as great as one hundred yards, not even an Olympic sprinter has a chance of getting away on foot.

People have, however, sometimes escaped the murderous intentions of enraged grizzlies by climbing a tree. There is a popular misconception that all bears can climb. Some species—such as the black bear in North America, the Asian sun bear, and the South American spectacled bear—are extremely nimble climbers. But the weight, build, and foot-and-claw structure of the grizzly prevents it from climbing, although cubs can scamper up trees, and a sow once was seen about ten feet up on a large cottonwood limb, trying to coax its cub down. Being a grizzly mother, in all likelihood she would have cuffed the cub out of the tree if she could have reached it.

I have personally witnessed the startling agility of grizzlies: their knack of balancing and walking along a low-leaning tree or fallen log, their ability to leap across a creek to avoid the bother of wading through it, and their high-jumping skill, which seems as improbable as the ability of a fat, stubby-winged bumblebee to fly. One spring day long ago, in a tidal inlet of the narrow Canadian coastal archipelago known as the Inside Passage, I attempted to canoe close to a beach-grazing grizzly as it munched skunk cabbage and aquatic weed that had washed ashore. "Close," of course, is a relative term, and I felt shielded by the water since grizzlies often wade but—unlike most other bear species—seldom swim. The attempt to get a fairly close picture of that bear would have been futile even if my camera, which wore no telescopic lens, had not bobbed up and down with me on the tidal swells. Bears have an acute sense of hearing, but my partner was careful with the paddle and I hardly think that bear heard us above the lapping of the waters. I think it was the even more acute sense of smell that warned the bear abruptly when the breeze shifted lightly, causing the animal to raise its head suddenly and see the movement on the choppy surface. The beach was narrow. Close behind the bear, a little bluff rose up at least a dozen feet high and almost sheer. The bear rose on its hind legs, facing us, hesitated for a moment to get our scent, then pirouetted with the grace of a ballet dancer. From that standing position, it effortlessly leaped atop the bluff and vanished into the rain forest.

I have mentioned the intelligence and unpredictability of bears, and that expedition furnished examples. One day at noon, having caught several trout, we put ashore on a tiny islet separated from the mainland by only thirty feet or so of waist-deep water, spitted our fish over a campfire, lunched sumptuously, and lay down on the mossy ground for a nap. My partner, awakened perhaps by a snapping twig or rolling gravel, nudged me awake just in time for us both to see a large, dark-coated grizzly wade out of the little channel and into the mainland brush. We found that it had crossed our islet, scattered and chewed at the scant remains of our fish, stepped lightly over my partner's sleeping body, and departed. It must have been attracted by the aroma of roasted trout, and it must have been somewhat disappointed at the meagerness of our leftovers, but it must also have decided that our human scent was less appetizing than that of trout—not worth the effort of a kill. It therefore left us unmolested, and we thanked our stars. Actually, we were incredibly lucky not to have awakened sooner. Any sudden movement probably would have doomed us.

On several successive days after that, I spotted a large, dark grizzly, its coat appearing frosted as it reflected the sun, warming itself and dozing on a high, open shoreside bluff above a sprawling tidal flat. I first became aware of its presence while scanning the bluff with my binoculars, and it seemed quite unaware of me. I decided to see if I could get as close as, say, two hundred yards or less, counting heavily on the reputedly dim eyesight of bears.

Three times, when the tide was sufficiently low for me to walk the tidal flat crouching low and even crawling as the distance between us narrowed, I attempted the stalk. On each occasion and regardless of wind direction, when I came within about three hundred yards, the bear sat up, swung its head from side to side to test the air for scent, then gazed directly toward me for perhaps half a minute, then retreated into the woods. I finally acknowledged defeat, feeling a trifle guilty for having disrupted the animal's peaceful sunning sessions,

I find it hard to believe that the bear saw me as it gazed down on the broad, sun-reflecting tidal flat. And if it did I cannot believe it distinguished me from the driftwood, stumps, boulders, and logs that dotted the expanse. Every time it sat up, I froze in position. I believe its sense of smell

told it everything it needed to know.

All the same, bears have better vision than is generally attributed to them. Begging bears in parks and zoos can catch a tossed bit of food in midair. During salmon runs on Alaskan and British Columbian streams, bears snap or cuff at leaping fish. Contrary to general belief, this is not their invariable method of catching salmon; they prefer the far more efficient technique of first pinning a fish to the stream bottom with one or both paws. Playing aerial catch with the salmon appears suspiciously like sport—and never let any expert tell you that mammals do not play for the sake of play. I suspect that the cuffing and snapping is mostly confined to the younger, less experienced bears. Though hardly cost-effective in terms of expended energy, the attempts at midair catching succeed. Any person who has tried to play this fish-capturing game will attest that it requires a combination of good vision and extremely fast reflexes. The bears mostly fail not because of deficient eyesight but because the squirming fish are too slippery for them to grip.

Further evidence of good ursine eyesight was furnished more than half a century ago in controlled zoo experiments proving that the captive brown bears recognized their keeper at one hundred yards. Though their vision hardly compares with that of deer or sheep, it is certainly not weak.

One author has theorized that the myth of poor vision stems from the habit bears have of averting their gaze during a nonaggressive encounter with other bears or humans. The averted gaze—a habit shared with some other predatory animals—is probably a signal or display of nonaggression, and when bears congregate at a food source, it may well be a display not merely of nonaggression but of submission when an animal is confronted by a large, dominant male or a female with yearling cubs. Perhaps this habit nurtured the myth, but observers of wild bears agree that bears simply have no need to utilize their eyes in the manner of some other animals. They appear to count more on scent and sound to locate either prey or a threat, while leaving their eyes in a state that might be called "unoccupied"—not sharply staring at or focusing on any particular detail but able to detect movement instantly. And when they hear or smell anything unfamiliar, they do use their eyes effectively to pinpoint the intrusion.

Reproduction and Denning

Another popular misconception merits correction here. Bears are not true hibernators, or perhaps it is more accu-

A BEAR HUNT IN THE ROCKY MOUNTAINS.

rate to state that are not deep hibernators. Woodchucks, or groundhogs, are true hibernators. When they go underground for the winter, they curl up tightly and fall into an extremely deep sleep from which it is almost impossible to rouse them. The body temperature of these marmots drops from almost ninety-seven degrees F to less than forty, and the metabolic changes are drastic. The heartbeat slows from over a hundred beats per minute to four, circulation slows, a breath is taken only once in about six minutes, all growth stops, and fat is absorbed for survival. The raccoon

also dens in winter and may become quite torpid, but does not hibernate. In fact, it will occasionally emerge during mild weather.

Bears in warm climates seldom if ever den. Bears in more northerly latitudes den, and undergo somewhat more pronounced metabolic changes than raccoons, becoming considerably more torpid, but they are much more closely comparable to the latter than to any deeply hibernating species. The black bear, for example, may take to its winter bed in response to the first heavy snowfall, and its metabolism will slow down somewhat, but it will sleep only intermittently. The timing of this phenomenon varies with both climate and species (and to some degree with individual animals), but scientists generally agree that denning is triggered in most species by some combination of several factors: satiation after autumnal gluttony—an instinctive gorging in preparation for winter—as well as a diminishing of food supplies with the onset of winter, and the shortening of daylight hours (the daylight-darkness ratio, which operates a biological "calendar" in many creatures, from certain insects to birds and mammals. Many black bears den regardless of snow, but a heavy fall may be a final prod for some. Be that as it may, they awaken frequently and occasionally emerge even in midwinter—except for pregnant females, which give birth in their sleep, usually in January.

Snowfall is an extremely unlikely triggering mechanism for polar bears, whose denning calendar is almost surely governed by a combination of lengthening darkness, accumulation of fat reserves, and the gradual withdrawal of

DANCING BEARS IN INDIA.—FROM A DRAWING BY W. CARPENTER, JUN.

available food in the form of seals, their primary and often sole prey. Male polar bears and females that are not pregnant seldom den at all for any extended period, but sometimes they apparently enter a moderately decelerated physiological state—"walking hibernation"—in which they remain awake most of the time and active. In October or early November (in at least some regions) pregnant females dig maternity dens in snow banks. Because snow is a fine insulator and the bear's body continually gives off heat, the den's air temperature may rise as high as forty degrees F when the outside temperature is below zero. They give birth in December or January. Although their metabolism slows somewhat more than that of black bears and they seem to go into a deeper sleep, they do occasionally emerge.

If changes in prevailing wind direction remove too much snow from the roof of the ursine igloo, the polar bear abandons it and either digs a new den or seeks out an old, vacant one. Some zoological reference works, such as the *Larousse Encyclopedia of Animal Life*, state that the "Polar Bear does not hibernate, though there has been some difference of opinion on this."

Brown bears are so widely distributed through Europe, Asia, and North America that the denning habits of the many subspecies necessarily vary to some extent—probably depending at least in large measure on regional climate and food availability. A great deal is known about the American form, the grizzly bear, as a result of pioneering studies carried out in Yellowstone Park by Doctors John and Frank Craighead and their associates. They found that a great many bears in the local population all denned at more or less the same time, typically during a storm or heavy snow in November.

Soon after denning, the metabolic rate is reduced and these bears become quite comatose. For as long as six months, such a bear usually will not leave the den unless disturbed, and it does not eat, defecate, urinate, or drink. Its nourishment and all the fluid it needs are taken from its autumnally accumulated layers of fat. Grizzly cubs are generally born in late January or early February—most often twins, as with other bear species. Although a grizzly seldom leaves its den before spring, it does awake occasionally, and will tinker with its bedding to achieve maximum warmth. If it has given birth, it may also groom its cubs.

For several days before denning, bears quit their ravenous foraging and, in fact, begin a total fast. By the time they retire, the stomach and intestines are quite empty, and the stomach contracts so drastically that it has been compared to the solidity of a bird's gizzard. During dormancy, a somewhat resinous fecal plug, or seal, forms in the lower colon, near the anus, closing off the alimentary tract. Its purpose, if any, is a matter of speculation. At one time, some observers suggested that bears indiscriminately consumed bits of coarse vegetation at the end of the active feeding period in order to form this plug, but that has been disproved. The bits of vegetation are merely waste scraps that have drained down from the lower intestine.

When bears first emerge from their dens, they often do little but walk about for a while, more or less aimlessly, apparently getting the stiffness out of their joints and reviving muscular control. Another reason for several days of seemingly aimless wandering may be to seek the first sproutings of green vegetation. They soon begin browsing and grazing on the lushest, most succulent vegetation they can find. Another long-held misconception (or at best, half-truth) was that this initial diet provided a laxative that helped to expel the plug. It may well have some laxative effect that helps to get the alimentary system working quickly, but it is not needed for any other reason. The plug is ejected easily when the bear becomes active, and even in winter is instantly expelled if a bear becomes sufficiently alarmed or disturbed to flee its den.

Among denning bears, the timing of gestation and birth is extremely important. Born in the den, which is always warmer than the outside air temperature, the young are further warmed by the mother as they press against its body, often encircled by its limbs, sometimes half buried in its winter-thick fur of long outer guard hairs and dense, insulating undercoat. They ingest their mother's very rich milk during the remainder of the winter (and long afterward). When the mother emerges in spring, the cubs have been crawling about the den for some time, occasionally venturing as far as the entrance, and they too are ready to emerge, toddling about, stumbling and rolling, awkwardly rushing to stay close.

This timing is achieved by a marvelous phenomenon known as delayed implantation. Among black bears and grizzlies (and many other subspecies of brown bear), mating occurs in June or July—a peak period of activity that is ideal for mating and allows a pregnant sow bear the full summer and autumn of optimal foraging. But without delayed implantation the young would be born too soon and might not survive the winter.

What happens is that the fertilized egg becomes a tiny embryo and undergoes the initial divisions common to mammals but temporarily ceases development and does not become attached to the uterine wall. Instead it floats free in the uterus in a kind of suspended animation until autumn and only then becomes implanted in the uterine wall. The precise timing of implantation and embryonic development depends upon species and region. In polar bears, the development resumes in September, a month or two before denning, and obviously proceeds very rapidly for such a large animal. In black bears, this implantation is usually delayed until November, and subsequent development is even faster.

Equally unusual is the ratio of newborn to adult weight, for bear cubs are astonishingly tiny. A couple of comparisons are in order to clarify the enormity of this ratio. In porcupines, the ratio averages 1:15—that is, the mother weighs fifteen times more than the infant. In humans, the ratio is 1:20. But if two newborn black bears each weighed a twentieth of their mother's weight—each scaling ten to fifteen pounds—the mother could not effectively nurse them. The mother probably would starve in the den, or else its cubs might starve. Therefore, newborn black bears are about the size of squirrels (tailless squirrels): about eight inches long and weighing perhaps six to ten ounces. The ratio of cub to mother size is thus about 1:500. A grizzly mother weighing 450 pounds has cubs weighing about ten ounces each, for a ratio of 1:750. A nine-hundred-pound polar bear is apt to produce twenty-ounce cubs, a ratio of about 1:725.

Initial infant growth is necessarily very rapid since weak and tiny cubs could not cope with emergence from the den. In a couple of months or so, they can easily gain twenty-five times their birth weight. Those same polar bears that weighed twenty ounces at birth may weigh over thirty pounds when they leave the den. When an infant black bear emerges from the den, it still weighs only about five pounds, having gained only eight to thirteen times its birth weight, but by the end of June it may weigh twenty-four pounds. Further details of breeding and denning—all equally intriguing—are found later in this book, in the separate discussions of several species.

Ursine Evolution

Because the fossil record is incomplete and intermittent, the early stages of bear evolution form a somewhat sketchy story. Paleontologists believe that the ancestors of modern bears began to evolve early in the Oligocene Epoch, some thirty to forty million years ago, as one of several groups branching from a family of carnivorous little tree climbers called miacids. From this same arboreal stock are descended a second group, the raccoons and coatis, and a third comprising the canines—wolves, foxes, coyotes, and dogs. Interestingly, all three modern groups—bears, raccoons, and canines—are exceptionally intelligent by comparison with most mammals, yet the ancestral miacids had small brains. This amounts to another ursine paradox. A possible explanation is the theory that prehistoric prey was relatively easy to capture, but in the ensuing millions of years some of the prey developed larger, better brains (an instance of natural selection in which the less intelligent were killed by predators while the smart escaped to reproduce). As the prey became smarter in order to escape the predators, the predators became smarter in order to catch the prey. Such theories may be speculative but seem quite logical.

Some paleontologists hold that the oldest known creature that legitimately could be called a bear was *Ursavus elemensis*, a predator the size of a small dog. It inhabited subtropical Europe some twenty million years ago. By about six million years ago, larger and more bearlike bears existed, and soon (soon, that is, in geological terms) developed into many forms, a few of them gigantic. Subsequently, however, many genera and many more species within those genera met extinction, probably doomed by changing climate and habitat. Our modern bears are thought to have descended from a small species, *Protursus*, which also became extinct. Between two and three million years ago the genus *Ursus* finally appeared. Its descendants splintered into three separate lineages, one in Europe that was the progenitor of the extinct cave bear, *U. spelaus*, and two in Asia that brought forth today's brown bears on three continents and the black bear in North America.

Fossilized bones of cave bears have been dated from about ten thousand to fifty thousand years ago, making them contemporary with prehistoric man. Cave men evidently hunted cave bears, and it is possible that cave bears hunted cave men. Then as now, the odds favored the humans. At Drachenloch Cave in the Swiss Alps, a crude stone coffer containing bear skulls was discovered. Perhaps they were prehistoric hunting trophies and were meant to bestow magic power on the hunters, as the trophies of dangerous game do among some primitive cultures today.

There is some paleontological controversy to the effect that cave bears may have been chiefly or even purely herbivorous, but it seems more likely that they were as omnivorous as modern bears.

Their common name is derived from the sites at which remains have been found. Probably they denned in caves, and there is no doubt that prehistoric human hunters brought many of the carcasses to their own caves for consumption. Many of the bones show scars inflicted by stone weapons or butchering tools or both.

In addition to skulls and skeletons found in Switzerland, Germany, and Hungary, enormous numbers were uncovered in Austria, particularly at a site known as the Dragon Cave in the early 1920s by workmen quarrying bat guano for fertilizer. A somewhat surprising percentage of infant bear skeletons provided fairly solid evidence that the bears denned in caves. Skeletal reconstructions and related analyses such as skull dimensions indicate that a large, mature male would have weighed nearly nine hundred pounds, the size of a polar bear or big Alaskan brown.

A similar but separate species, known as the Florida cave bear, existed in America, ranging from the Gulf Coast across Florida and northward into Tennessee. In 1983, the discovery of a very large canine tooth in South Dakota led to the realization that another prehistoric bear existed on this continent, and it was even larger. Confirmation was provided by fossil discoveries elsewhere, proving that this Ice Age bear was distributed from Alaska to Mexico and from California eastward across the continent to Virginia. This species, *Arctodus simus*, had a short, broad muzzle and has been given the common name short-faced bear.

This was probably the largest of all the Ice Age bears. It stood more than five feet high at the shoulder and was at least fifteen percent larger than today's Alaskan grizzlies. It had long legs and very powerful musculature. Everything about the fossils indicates that the short-faced bear was a swift predator that could bring down large prey. This is hardly surprising, for modern grizzlies have occasionally killed horses and domestic cattle, and they have been known to kill full-grown moose.

Most of the present forms of bears have probably been in existence for less than a million years. American black bears evidently came from Asian ancestors and were well established long before grizzlies came to America. The earliest brown bears—direct ancestors of those now existing—are thought to have occurred in China. They spread through Asia and Europe, but it was not until the Ice Age that they apparently crossed the Bering Strait land bridge to North America. Youngest of the modern species is the polar bear, which evidently evolved from brown bears on or near the Siberian coast. Estimates of this species' age range from a little more than a quarter of a million years ago to a mere one hundred thousand years. Its numbers eventually spread around the globe to achieve circumpolar distribution, but only in arctic and subarctic latitudes where vegetation was sparse or absent. Gradually adapting to such habitat, it was forced to develop specialized feeding habits and thus became the most truly carnivorous of the bear family.

Bears in Legend, Literature, and Art

Man's fascination with bears has found expression for many thousands of years. Some of Europe's eave paintings depict bearlike creatures, probably early brown bears but possibly cave bears. The ancients perceived bearlike shapes in the heavens and named the constellations containing the Big Dipper and Little Dipper Ursa Major and Ursa Minor. Some of the native American peoples referred to bears as their relatives—grandfathers, grandmothers, brothers, and the like. Depending upon region and tribe, this indicated either a belief in supernatural kinship between species or in reincarnation as animals that exhibited humanlike postures and behavior. There were legends of transmutation—people-bears and bear-people—and even a few instances of taboos against killing bears. Among the Dakotas, a boy's puberty rites included remaining for several days in a pit called a bear hole, fasting and imitating a bear.

In the arenas of ancient Rome, bears were pitted against dogs and gladiators. The Greco-Roman attitude was curiously ambivalent, for bears were revered as symbols of strength, kept for amusement in the menageries of rulers, and savagely killed for sport in the arena. The latter practice persisted for many centuries, though the precise form of brutality changed, as the animals were pitted against trained bear-baiting dogs in Europe and England. Although the Puritans disapproved of such bloody spectacles, European settlers and explorers were astonished by native cultures that embraced bear clans, ascribed magic powers to bears, and perpetuated legends such as that of a boy raised by a sow bear and a woman whose lover was a bear. The scoffing, superior stance of the settlers now seems ironic in view of their own heritage, which included animalistic myths about Leda and the swan, the she-wolf that suckled Romulus and Remus, and so on.

European culture also nurtured the tradition of oral folktales of miraculous animals, including bears. In Charles Perrault's *Tales of Mother Goose*, a 1697 work based faithfully on oral tradition, the beast in "Beauty And the Beast" may have evolved from tales of bears or bearish men. The *Kinder-und Hausmarchen* of the Brothers Grimm, transcribed from oral renderings in 1812-1815, included a fairy tale about a penniless soldier who was forced by a demon to shoot an immense bear and wear its skin for seven years. For keeping his vow to wear the skin and submit to other penances—while remaining a good person all the while—he was rewarded with money and ultimately a beautiful bride.

In another Grimm story, a haughty princess tells a tailor she will agree to marry him if he can live through a night in a stable occupied by a ferocious bear. The tailor tricks the bear (a talking, dancing bear, by the way) into putting its paw into the jaws of a vise which, of course, the tailor immediately tightens. In the morning, while he and the princess ride in a coach to the church where they will be married, the tailor's two jealous brothers free the enraged bear. With the bear in close pursuit, the clever tailor sticks his legs through the coach window and tells the bear they are another vise which will catch and hold him forever. This frightens the bear away, and the tailor and the princess live happily ever after.

Probably the most popular of all such tales is "Goldilocks and the Three Bears." I would not be surprised to learn that every child of my generation read or listened to it, and during the past decade at least eight hardcover editions were in print in the United States, including one accompanied by an audiocassette and one in sign language.

The prehistoric cave bears described earlier were the basis for folktales and legends of a very different kind, involving a belief in dragons. Among the sites where the bones of cave bears accumulated were Drachenloch in Switzerland and the Drachenfels in Germany—the so-called dragon's caves. The skulls, considerably larger than those of present-day European bears and characterized by a steeply sloping forehead, gave rise to legends of dragons, and the size of the body and leg bones reinforced a belief in such creatures. It was at the Drachenfels in the Sieben Gebirge that Siegfried was supposed to have slain his dragon. In the midnine-teenth century, Richard Wagner, having studied Norse myths and the German Siegfried legend, wrote the poems and musical dramas that coalesced into *Der Ring des Nibelungen*. Thus did bears furnish—however indirectly—part of the inspiration for Wagnerian opera.

Bears, or rather a specific black bear, furnished the inspiration for one of the world's most popular playthings, the Teddy Bear. Theodore Roosevelt, twenty-sixth president of the United States, was an enthusiastic hunter and naturalist, and an ardent conservationist as well. In 1902 he captured a black bear cub during one of his expeditions and for a while kept it as a pet. A doll manufacturer named Morris Michton used the cub as a model for the first Teddy Bear, so named with Roosevelt's blessing.

A live bear was also enlisted in the longest-lasting and most famous advertising campaign in behalf of conservation and woodland safety in the United States. In 1944, the U.S. Forest Service featured Walt Disney's little animated cartoon deer, *Bambi*, on a poster promoting forest-fire prevention. The success of the poster prompted the Forest Service to create its own symbolic animal as a fire-prevention theme, and Smokey the Bear was created. The character was named after a former assistant chief of New York's Fire Department, "Smokey Joe" Martin.

Then, in the fall of 1950, a real bear became the mascot and living symbol for the poster campaign. My friend Jack Samson, who was then public relations director for the New Mexico Department of Game & Fish, has furnished the details of the story. Crews of Forest Service personnel and Mescalero Indians were fighting a major forest fire in New Mexico's White Mountains when they found a small black bear perched on a smoldering ponderosa pine stump. In escaping the fire it had run over burning coals, severely scorching all four of its feet. The mother could not be found. Either the fire had killed the sow or the inferno had separated it from the cub.

Ray Bell, the game department's law-enforcement chief, flew the cub to Santa Fe, where a veterinarian medicated and bandaged its paws. The bear stayed briefly at the Bell home, where it bit Ray Bell's small daughter and tried to kill the family cocker spaniel. Next it was lodged at the Game Department's Santa Fe office, where the public came to view it. However, the pain and terror it had experienced had made it a permanently mean and dangerous animal, and it tried to bite anyone who came near it. The question now was what to do with the pathetic but menacing creature.

Jack Samson discussed it with Morgan Smith, the Forest Service public affairs chief in Santa Fe. They decided the cub would make a splendid mascot and symbol for the poster and advertising campaign cautioning and educating the public about careless acts that can start forest fires. After all, the posters already featured a drawing of a bear wearing a ranger hat and uttering the message, "Only you can prevent forest fires." Forest Service headquarters in Washington, D.C., enthusiastically agreed and had the cub shipped to the Washington Zoo, where the public was encouraged to visit it. Inevitably and promptly, they named him Smokey.

This live personification of the Smokey symbol was a popular attraction and undoubtedly benefited the cause, but the bear remained a problem for many years, until it eventually died. It repeatedly attacked its keepers and tried to kill the female black bears that were introduced to it in the hope that the bear would mate. Smokey has always been pictured in advertisements and on posters as a benevolent, fatherly bear. "What a sad irony," Jack commented to me, "that the live Smokey had a temperament forged in the torment of fire and was one of the meanest black bears that ever existed."

From Winnie-the-Pooh to Yogi Bear, the ursine characters of this century's children's fiction provide a delightfully kindly contrast.

Bear Species

An animal that is very bearlike in appearance, the panda, sometimes called panda bear, is absent from this book and most others concerning ursine species. Although many people assume the panda is a true bear, its taxonomic classification remains in debate—a dispute rekindled in recent years. Like bears, it is descended from the miacids, and it was first described by the naturalist Pere David as belonging to the bear group, but in spite of its resemblance to a Teddy Bear, the differences are striking. Although it eats meat (as do a number of herbivores), if meat is presented to it and no hunting effort is involved the animal is herbivorous, subsisting on bamboo almost exclusively. Unlike bears, it has a modified wrist bone that forms a sixth digit—functioning rather like a thumb—on its forepaws, allowing it to handle bamboo shoots and leaves with impressive dexterity. Scientists have long regarded it as more closely allied to raccoons (also descended from miacids) than to bears, and not very closely related to either group.

Recent morphological and genetic research indicates that pandas are more closely related to bears, after all—or at least one species is. The chromosomes of the giant panda, plus other clues used by molecular biologists, indicate that it shares its lineage with bears, while the chromosomes of the red panda indicate that it is related to raccoons. The controversy continues, and it will be no surprise if taxonomists eventually agree to keep pandas in their own unique classification, separate from the true bears.

Even within the genera of true bears, scientists do not always find themselves in complete agreement about species. Earlier in this century, they divided brown bears into at least three distinct species, the European (or Eurasian) brown bear, the Alaskan (or Kodiak) brown bear, and the inland (or interior) grizzly. Now they classify these as a single species, in which case more than fifty subspecies of brown bear may be scattered across the world. This is not really surprising, since there are some eighteen subspecies, or geographic races, of the American black bear, a couple of which show little resemblance in coloration to the prototypical black bear. The following is a list of the bears in this book—the various species on which there is general agreement:

American Black Bear (*Ursus americanus*)
Asian Black, or Moon, Bear (*Selenarctos thibetanus*)
Brown Bear, including Alaskan Brown and Grizzly Bear (*Ursus arctos*)
Polar Bear (*Ursus maritimus*)
Sloth, or Indian, Bear (*Melursus ursinus*)
Spectacled, or Andean, Bear (*Tremarctos ornatus*)
Sun, or Malayan, Bear (*Helarctos malayanus*)

A black bear has led her cubs to a firewood pile behind a cabin. She has probably grown accustomed to human habitation and lost at least some of her fear. If disturbed, she may flee with her young, or attack to protect them.

1.
THE HUMAN FACTOR: CONFLICT AND CONSERVATION

Any thoughtful observer can draw wry amusement from the convergent similarity of human and bear reactions to unwelcome stimuli. A person who detects the presence or approach of something unpleasant or alarming may investigate, or at least hesitate long enough to confirm the nature of the intrusion, and will then either avoid it or attempt to drive it off—precisely as a bear does. A bear that perceives a more immediate threat to itself, its young, or a food supply may flee if sufficiently frightened or if escape appears easy, but is at least as likely to attack and either kill or scare off the intruder. This is precisely what humans have done when bears threatened them, their children, their livestock, or even, in some parts of the world, their orchards or yam fields.

Historically, the major difference has been that whereas bears could kill or maim individual victims or even develop the habit of killing livestock—easy prey—humankind was better equipped to wipe out whole populations of bears and has frequently done so in long-lasting vendettas. Fortunately, such vengeful slaughter is largely a crime of the past, except in parts of Asia, but tragic individual conflicts persist where bears encounter people.

The skepticism of some self-styled authorities notwithstanding, bears (especially grizzlies) have been known to trail and stalk people, probably in an effort to determine whether the strange two-legged animal was a competitor for food or some new variety of prey. Bud Branham, a pioneering Alaskan guide, has written about an angler he led to a favorite pool on a remote stream. After making a few casts, the angler had the sensation of being watched. Glancing up at the high stream bank, he saw a large grizzly staring down at him. The angler, who was terrified of bears, fled downstream at a laborious, high-splashing run, shouting to the guide for help, while the bear retreated into the woods. The guide then led the fisherman to another pool, perhaps a quarter mile away. With silent caution and determination, the bear circled through the woods and appeared again on the bank above the increasingly nervous angler. So persistent was the bear that the two men finally felt compelled to abandon the stream and fish other waters.

A bear standing upright like this Alaskan
brown may or may not be aggressive.
It rises to get an unobstructed view and
catch more scent and sound.

Such accounts have been fairly common, but still more common is the kind of experience I once had when I attempted to trail a bear (in this instance a black bear, identifiable by its tracks) along the edge of a British Columbian stream. The bear obviously knew it was being followed, and it could have—might have—circled around to come at me from behind. Instead, it simply kept retreating. I managed to get close enough twice to hear it crashing through brush, and once I got a fleeting glimpse of black fur almost screened by trees. Finally it veered away from the stream and escaped into the dense forest.

Many people who spend considerable time in bear country carry firearms for protection. In skilled hands, a sufficiently powerful firearm is, more often than not, a very efficient last resort. A Northwest Territories safety manual advises the reader not to shoot prematurely, because a bear's charge may be a bluff—in which case the bear will turn away—and because a shot at close range is both more accurate and more likely to have sufficient shocking effect to fell the animal. The first shot is often crucial; if the bear is broadside, the aim should be to the shoulder or low neck, but the animal will more likely be coming head on, in which case the aim should be for the center of the neck, low between the shoulders. Aiming for the head does not always have the necessary effect.

For many people, the use of a firearm is either impractical or distasteful. Some people carry shotguns loaded with harmless but noisy blanks—firecracker shells—to scare off aggressive bears. And some carry blank-firing starter pistols like those used at athletic events, but my personal opinion is that the pistol charges are not nearly loud enough. A newer and more effective deterrent is a chemical spray can, which is locally available in some areas where bears are prevalent (and also available from some companies by mail order). Most if not all of these sprays con-

This is an often-repeated scene when polar bears gather at Churchill. If one of the vehicle's lower windows were open, the bear would almost certainly reach a paw through it.

tain oil of red pepper, which evidently stings and disorients a bear, harmlessly, but with sufficient effect to turn aside a rush more often than not. Still, the best preventive is common-sense caution.

Historically—and currently, for that matter—the depletion and even the annihilation of some bear populations is not a direct and therefore somewhat understandable (though not pardonable) reaction to homicide. It has occurred and still does out of groundless fear or, in many regions, to protect livestock. Quite understandably, any bear may be tempted by easy prey. Investigations have, however, indicated that old or injured bears most often become the rogue killers of domestic animals. A bear with worn or broken teeth, an injured jaw, or crippled foot is likely to be a hungry bear that has difficulty foraging.

An angry or unhappy bear will often give ample warning of its intentions. It will frequently hold its head low, ready to charge. It may rise up on its hind legs to inspect an intruder, then come down again to make a rush. It may cough or woof, salivate or click its teeth and make a popping sound. But when the intention is to feed on cattle or sheep, the owner of the livestock receives no warning and has no knowledge of disaster until too late. Vengeance is the probable aftermath.

Grievously often, bears have been perceived as vermin or dreaded enemies of human society.

A polar bear, having grown accustomed to human presence, stretches for a look into a visitors' dormitory.

Churchill, Manitoba, is a renowned gathering place of polar bears waiting for pack ice to form so they can hunt seals. It is also a popular denning area. Signs here warn visitors not to invade the privacy of feeding bears.

The Bible (Isaiah 59:11) laments that "we roar all like bears, and mourn sore like doves." Man has had a fearfully adversarial relationship with bears, exhibited even in the implications of such labels as the "bears" of the stock exchange. On the European Continent and in Britain, brown bears were relentlessly hunted for centuries. By the Middle Ages they were gone from Britain, and by the midnineteenth century they survived only in small, remnant populations throughout most of Europe, although they probably remained somewhat more plentiful in the vast wilderness areas of Russia.

At present, Russia still has more bears than other European nations; even without counting the bears of Soviet Asia. In relative terms, Rumania also has a large population—perhaps four thousand. There are some bears in Yugoslavia, Czechoslovakia, and the Scandinavian countries, and a few—very few—in the French and Spanish Pyrenees. A few of these nations permit stringently controlled hunting, but the various governments are at the same time conducting habitat and wildlife management programs whose purposes include an increase in bear numbers. It cannot be denied that bears, despite their reduced populations, occasionally prey on domestic sheep and even cattle but, rather than allowing any further reduction in bear numbers, several countries now pay compensation to livestock owners. A program has been undertaken to reintroduce bears into the French Alps, and in the Carpathians, where bears inflict considerable timber damage, Soviet management centers on mitigating such damage rather than extirpating the animals.

East and northeast of the Mediterranean, in remote areas of Syria and Turkey, a few brown

Near the Yellowstone River, a large boar grizzly approaches the photographer on a bear trail. Fortunately, the bear is fully aware of the human. Surprise causes alarm, which may trigger flight or deadly attack. But in many parts of the world, the bears are in greater need of protection than the humans.

bears may yet exist, but they are gone from the Atlas Mountains of northern Africa. There are scattered populations of brown bears across Asia all the way to the Siberian coast and nearby islands, and the numbers may be considerable in some areas, but reliable figures are unavailable.

Neither in the Old World nor the New is the brown bear in danger of extinction. North America's brown bears, including the grizzlies, number about fifty thousand, chiefly in Alaska and in Canada's Yukon and Northwest Territories, British Columbia, and Alberta. Apart from Alaska, where the bears are plentiful, the United States probably has fewer than eight hundred, almost all of them in Yellowstone Park. Of course, the bears do not recognize park boundaries,

Although the American black bear is not usually as quick tempered as the brown, its reactions are unpredictable and should always be treated with great caution. This one has caught a fish and is about to eat its kill. Any bear guarding food should be regarded as dangerous.

and there is an old, continuing controversy over whether Montana should permit controlled hunting. The argument in favor of limited sport hunting is that it prevents an increase in livestock losses without having any effect on the apparently stable bear population.

In Canada and the United States, black bears are far more widespread and abundant—and a few are found as far south as Mexico, where the southerly race of grizzlies is now gone. Thirty years ago, probably no more than a couple of dozen wild bears remained in New Jersey. Then, in the early 1970s, hunting was stopped and effective management measures were inaugurated; within sixteen years the bear population had risen to about sixty, and since then has continued to grow at an accelerated rate.

Elsewhere, the bears are faring even better. There are good numbers in New England, the Southeast, the Midwest, and the Rockies. Owing to excellent management policies, the Pennsylvania bear population has doubled in less than two decades. Well-timbered states like Wisconsin and Michigan are known for their very large black bears. The State of New York has healthy populations in the Catskills and Adirondacks. Estimates for Washington State vary between thirty thousand and sixty thousand, which indicates a lot of bears even if the minimum figure is accepted.

This bear is far from endangered, but parts taken from Asian and American black bears are difficult or impossible to tell apart. Unscrupulous traders claim that bear parts in their possession come from American black bears, not subject to CITES regulation. The unregulated status of the American black bears therefore contributes to the threats to endangered Asian bears. In April of 1991, a shipment of 173 black bear galls was seized at Anchorage International Airport before two Alaska dealers could get it airborne to the Orient. The World Wildlife Fund and other conservation organizations are working hard with CITES—as well as the International Union for the Conservation of Nature (IUCN) and other agencies to curtail this trafficking.

Many bears have been killed so that their cubs could be captured and trained for circus use. Another form of exploitation is poaching for furs, as well as for parts used in medicines, aphrodisiacs, and the bear paw soup prized in the Orient.

Tour vehicles have stopped where a sow grizzly is about to lead her cubs across the road. Stepping out of a vehicle at such a time invites a tragedy that cannot be blamed on the bear.

This grizzly is baring its teeth in a threat display. It does not necessarily mean an attack is imminent, but it should he warning enough to any intruder.

2.
AMERICA'S UBIQUITOUS BLACK BEAR

There are eighteen subspecies of black bear, distributed throughout Canada and Alaska (except in the highest latitudes) and down the coasts of the United States to Florida and lower California, across the Great Lakes states and the forested portions of the Gulf Coast, and down through the Rockies into Arizona, New Mexico, western Texas, and northern Mexico. Thus, black bears occur in all of the Canadian provinces and in most of the continental United States, except for portions of the Southwest and lower Midwest, making them the continent's most widespread and successful ursine species. They are absent primarily in arid regions of sparse vegetation and where some of their original range was floated away by loggers.

Good habitat may be anywhere from sea level into the upper coniferous zones, although black bears seldom tarry for long above an elevation of seven thousand feet. They fare best in relatively open forests where dense hideaway thickets are interspersed with more open spaces that provide fruits and grasses. For most subspecies, ideal habitat has mixed stands of conifers and hardwoods, and drinking water in the form of streams, ponds, or lakes. Such habitat is fortunately common in the upper United States, and black bears are especially abundant in such states as Alaska, Washington, Oregon, Minnesota (and the entire Great Lakes region), Idaho, Colorado, North Carolina, and Maine. The continent's total population probably hovers around 750,000.

Although black bears in the Midwest and West tend to be larger than those in the East, there is no great size difference among the various geographic races or subspecies. However, a single subspecies or an individual bear may exhibit a great variation in size during a single season. Before denning in early winter, a yearling cub (about ten months old) may weigh as little as thirty or as much as ninety-five pounds; the following autumn, it is likely to weigh between eighty and 130 pounds; in its third year it will probably weigh between 215 and 295, and may reach its maximum weight the following year. Averages can be misleading. Some authorities state that an average, fully mature black bear weighs a little over three hundred pounds, while others prefer cautious weight-range figures—two hundred to four hundred pounds for a well-fed adult.

Poised atop a moss-carpeted boulder above a creek where spawning salmon are moving upstream, a black bear eyes the photographer. If the photographer remains still or retreats, an attack is unlikely, but the bear's head is sufficiently lowered to warrant great caution.

These photographs show a young black bear jumping a creek at a favorite spot and then leaping across a flooded trail. Black bears can swim—and often enjoy doing so—but tend to jump across narrow, shallow passages that a less nimble animal would have to wade. From a slow walk or standing position, they can jump surprisingly high and far. The almost furless patch on this animal's side is from normal springtime shedding, not illness or injury.

Glossy and fat in early fall, this black bear has the typical coloration of the species in the Eastern and Midwestern United States, black with a pale tan muzzle and whitish chest blaze.

A black bear and a cougar engage in battle, almost certainly over the carcass of prey one of them has killed. The engagement will be brief, and the cougar will flee.

A coyote is no match for a black bear guarding food or cubs. The coyote in this case has realized its mistake.

Statistics fail to convey an accurate image of the black bear, because males are much larger than females, and a number of boar bears have weighed more than six hundred pounds and measured nine feet from nose to rump. (The tail length counts for nothing since this stubby little appendage is generally held down flat and is almost unnoticeable in the thick fur.) The heaviest recorded weight I have found was that of a Wisconsin black bear killed in 1885. It scaled 802 pounds, which would be closer to normal for an Alaskan brown bear. The largest black bear skull I have located on record was found in Utah in 1975; it was 14¾ inches long, 8⅞ inches wide. In more recent years, bears closely comparable to that one have been recorded in Utah, Arizona, and Saskatchewan.

I once heard a visitor at a zoo comment to her young daughter that the black bears in the enclosure must be smaller than those in the wild—perhaps stunted by captivity. After all, the largest of them stood only about three feet high at the shoulder and perhaps a trifle higher at the middle of its rounded back. Actually, that bear weighed about three hundred pounds and was in excellent condition. Their legs are relatively short for their thick bodies. Typical length from nose to rump is four to five feet or a little more, so observers are apt to be startled when a

At one time, black bears of different hues were thought to be separate species. This is a chocolate-brown black bear with coal-black cubs.

31

This two-month-old cub may not weigh much more than five pounds, but that may be ten times its birth weight.

bear stands upright on its hind legs, bringing its eyes about on a level with their own.

Transplanted Europeans, who were aware only of their continent's brown bears and white polar bears, understandably named this New World species the black bear, for that was invariably the color phase they saw during the early years of exploration and colonization. In the East and Midwest, nearly all bears have a glossy black coat with a tan or grizzled muzzle; dark brown, almost black eyes; and quite often a white chest blaze. But color variations become progressively more common to the west, often occurring among siblings. Black bears may, in fact, be black, brown, tan, or a paler tan sometimes described as blond or rusty brown. The rusty ones were long regarded as a separate species, called cinnamon bears. True albinism is very rare among bears,

The habit of standing upright begins very early, almost as soon as cubs become surefooted and can balance without tottering. This one has risen to its full height to peer over knee-high wildflowers.

Climbing a tree is easy: a cub reaches upward with its forepaws and clings to the trunk while the hind legs work like pistons to push the body up. Returning to the ground is harder and less graceful: coming down backwards—rump first—the process is almost a controlled fall.

While one cub rests momentarily, its sibling stands upright to search its mother's ear for wood ticks. Ticks cling mightily, but the cub can pull them off with its teeth.

but in one small locale a subspecies—still brown of eye and grayish black of nose—is about as white coated as a polar bear, and a subspecies in another, even smaller locale is most often bluish gray. All of these are variations of the same species, *Ursus americanus.*

The white variety, known as the Kermode bear (*U. a. kermodei*), is found in several small, isolated pockets of more or less coastal habitat in upper west-central British Columbia. Hunting them is strictly prohibited. Their numbers are uncertain, but probably they are not abundant and unquestionably they are elusive—in fact, seldom seen. The native people refer to these white phantoms of the northern rain forest as ghost bears. They were first described scientifically in 1905 by William Hornaday, an eminent naturalist and conservationist. Understandably regarding them as a distinct species, he named them after Francis Kermode, a Canadian colleague who had secured data and specimens for him. The first quarter of this century was marked by significant advances in taxonomy (though not quite comparable to the spurt of discoveries in this last

These are twin cubs in Washinton's well forested Cascade Mountains. Black is the normal color here, and is almost invariable, but brown or cinnamon is more common to the south in upper California.

Although black bears cannot rival the skill of browns at catching fish, they often manage to catch weakly swimming salmon and trout in shallow water during spawning runs.

This cinnamon-coated bear, standing upright to test the air for scent, is typical of black bears in California's Sierra Mountains.

Bears often fashion daybeds by raking leaves and twigs into a mat hidden in brush or thick woods. But these animals are unpredictable, and individual habits vary drastically. This one is sleeping soundly on open ground in a cedar swamp.

quarter), and in 1928 scientists confirmed a suspicion that the Kermode bear was simply an unusual white geographic race of black bear.

The other uniquely colored race is the glacier bear, or blue bear (*U. a. emmonsii*), which is found only in southeastern Alaska's St. Elias Range, more specifically on the coast of Yakutat Bay. A typical glacier bear is of medium size and has a luxuriant bluish gray coat, but the hue is quite variable. My friend Bud Branham, who was a pioneering Alaskan guide, says he has seen specimens ranging from frosted or silvery black to a glistening, almost midnight blue color. These bears are found only along a coastal mountainous strip less than a hundred miles long. At first, naturalists thought these animals, too, were a distinct species but, like the Kermode bears, they were proved by studies in comparative taxonomy to be but another color phase.

Descended from tree-climbing carnivores and normally inhabiting forested areas, black bears have a life-long ability to climb trees, but do so infrequently after reaching maturity—and the

Deep in the forest in summer, these bears are mating—an act seldom witnessed. Though solitary at other times, they may travel and forage together for as long as a month during the breeding season.

These companions are probably siblings in their second year. After leaving their mother, they may remain together for another year.

Reflections and the angle of light make this Kermode bear look tawnier than it actually is, but there is a good possibility that the animal is the product of interbreeding between two subspecies.

Depending on the angle of the sun, a Kermode bear may appear tinged with pink or gray. In addition, some of them interbreed with black bears of more typical coloration, which may result in an intergrading of characteristics.

At first glance, this strange animal might be taken for a polar bear somehow transplanted from the arctic to a rain forest. It is a white black bear, the rare Kermode subspecies found only in central and upper British Columbia near the coast.

In the forest above Glacier Bay, a blue bear nibbles buds and twigs while also keeping an alert watch for any unexpected movement that might betray a competitor, prey, or the human enemy.

This beautiful gray creature, subtly tinged with bluish overtones, is a typical specimen of the blue bear, or glacier bear, a subspecies of the black found only along one short segment of Alaska's southeastern coast.

Late in the afternoon, amid lengthening shadows, a big male pauses on a bear trail that meanders across a meadow. Although bears wander over large areas, they often establish well-worn trails to particular destinations such as drinking water, berry patches, or trees with rich, juicy cambium.

bigger the bear, the less inclined it is to climb. One can assume that a four-hundred-pound animal has great difficulty shinnying up a tree. The smaller ones do so to reach a honey-laden bees' nest, fruit, or a concentration of insect larvae, and cubs climb merely to play or explore. A tree is also a safe retreat, a primary means of defense for cubs and juveniles.

A black bear's claws are shorter and much more deeply curved than those of a grizzly, and this adaptation aids in gripping. Climbing is one of the first things a cub learns to do, and it is done with the hind feet. The forepaws merely grip and prevent a fall, while the hind feet are brought up under the belly and then straightened—"extended like pistons," as the naturalist Joe Van Wormer expressed it—after which the forepaws reach up for a higher hold. A hurrying bear will clamber straight up; otherwise, it will spiral up around the trunk. Coming down again is a more difficult procedure, awkward enough to be amusing to an observer. Although a bear may leap down from a low limb if it decides to leave the scene quickly, the normal method is to back down, almost falling, its paws gripping momentarily here and there and raking the bark to keep from dropping too quickly. The animal generally lets go entirely when it is a few feet from the ground, landing heavily on its haunches.

Grown bears are solitary animals with little tolerance for their own kind. There have been stories of females with cubs adopting an additional, orphaned cub, but adults tend to avoid one another except at mating time or when a concentration of food attracts several to one place. Even a large two-year-old is apt to run away or retreat up a tree at the approach of a strange adult, especially if the adult is a good-sized male or a female with cubs. It knows its enemies.

The mating season is from June through July. As it begins, males wander farther than usual, seeking females, and the females seem to extend their wanderings slightly, too. Although a black bear may remain in a very small area as long as it provides plenty of food, the species is not strongly territorial; in some regions the average home range may be only five square miles, while in others it may be many times as large. When a male finds a receptive female, the pair will feed and travel together amicably. In fact, for about a month they demonstrate great affection. And then they go their separate ways.

Owing to the phenomenon of delayed implantation, the fertilized egg produces an embryo that does not begin to grow and develop until fall. Denning time is as early as October in Alaska, but at least a month later over most of the range. There is no such thing as a typical black bear den; it may be a cave, a recess under a ledge, a sheltered hollow among boulders, the space

Bears shed heavily in springtime, and during this molt they seem to be plagued by itching. Sometimes a bear will adopt a favorite rubbing tree. This brownish-black bear is scratching its back against a tree in South Carolina.

Bears are surprisingly dexterous as well as intelligent. Here, a yearling black bear bends a sapling and uses it as a back scratcher, although not in this instance to alleviate an itch. Black bears are not very strongly territorial, but they will rub trees and other objects as a scent-marking ritual.

In Yellowstone National Park, a black bear rests before resuming its feast of mule deer. It probably found the deer already dead, since an adult deer in good health can easily outrun a bear.

On a hot summer day, a black bear plays and wallows in a cool, secluded pond. Afterward, the animal may violently shake itself like a dog to get rid of some of the water trapped in its fur.

All bears have long tongues and put them to use in licking up grubs and other small morsels. They also use their tongues, as this one is doing, to extract honey, honeycomb, and larvae from bees' nests. If necessary, they will also smash a nest, though cubs have been observed running away when stung.

At the edge of a meadow, a bear munches clusters of coralberries. Bears are exceedingly fond of ripe berries and, later in the fall, acorns, beech nuts, and any other available foods.

beneath the upheaved root mass of a fallen tree, the ground under a drooping conifer, or a hollow log or tree. Some bears dig holes in hillsides or under stumps or logs, some merely bed down in brushy tangles, and occasionally in settled country they take shelter in small culverts. In cold regions with little snow, a southern exposure is favored, but north slopes are often preferred where they are likely to accumulate deep snow drifts. Snow furnishes excellent insulation and concealment. A bear may scoop out earth to enlarge its den, rake in a mat or screen of twigs and leaves, or attempt no home improvements at all.

Sow bears breed only in alternate years. The following spring, the mother will be receptive again to a male, and when one comes along will ignore or even rebuff its yearlings. At first confused and perhaps distressed, they may attempt to linger very briefly. But by now they are self-sufficient, and do not long tolerate the mother's indifference or the intimidation that the mother's new suitor almost invariably displays. A lone yearling simply leaves. If there are two, they usually move on together and remain together for another year, finally separating when they are about two and a half years old to become solitary creatures, like older bears. A year later they are sexually mature, whether male or female, and ready to relinquish solitude just long enough to participate in another renewal of the life cycle.

This black bear has sat down to rest on a low slope, probably drowsily digesting a morning's repast. A mature male, he is not merely fat but actually huge.

A cinnamon-colored sow attacks a jet-black male that has ventured too near her cubs. The boar bear probably intended no harm, but females know instinctively that an adult male is a lethal threat to small cubs.

A plump young California bear eyes a rotted tree crevice that may hold a rich feast of insects. To get at them, the bear may rip away bark or gouge out big chunks of the soft wood, a procedure simplified by long, curved claws and very powerful muscles.

Adult black bears (except perhaps for the very heaviest of them) retain the ability to climb trees, and climbing is one of the first things a mother teaches her young because trees provide a safe retreat. This one has ascended with her cubs, an incentive for them to stay up there for a while.

Yearling cubs play among the upper branches of a tree in spring. Such activity probably helps to limber them up after an inactive winter in cramped quarters.

Bears are not true hibernators, and they sometimes seem to be impervious to cold. This one may have wallowed in a half-frozen creek, for it has icy winter mud frozen to its fur.

A black bear in southeastern Alaska pauses in its foraging to gaze at an intruder. It is using its ears and nose as well as its eyes to determine if the alien presence is a threat, a competitor, prey, or something too inconsequential to warrant action. The difficulty for wildlife photographers is that bears' decisions in these matters tend to be unpredictable.

This bear appears to have backed into a crevice among boulders banking a stream in order to waylay fish running upstream to spawn. The cavelike lair, catching the spray of a stream that may not freeze and situated where insulating snow may not accumulate, is useful for temporary concealment or shelter but will not be chosen for winter denning.

3.

SOUTH AMERICA'S SPECTACLED BEAR

The spectacled bear exists in scattered populations from Venezuela southward through the Andes into southern Peru and northernmost Chile. Also known as the Andean bear, it is South America's only ursine species.

Black and roughly the same size and weight as North America's black bear, but perhaps a trifle leaner, it is a handsome creature with extremely variable facial coloration. Often it has large, ringlike "spectacles" ranging from white to tawny, extending from the whitish or mottled snout up and around the eyes. On some individuals the pale color is absent or broken—oversized eyebrows rather than eyeglasses—or may spread to form a mask. It may also extend down and outward, forming a rim along the jowls. Frequently it spills down to form a small, whitish chest blaze.

This glossy black creature is by no means the South American counterpart of North America's black bear. During the last Ice Age, a giant short-faced bear roamed over both continents. The spectacled bear, thought to be descended from that prehistoric species or one much like it, is the only survivor of a subfamily of short-faced bears.

Most spectacled bears inhabit steep, thickly forested mountain slopes, having been exiled by civilization from the lowland savannas and foothills. Some, however, remain on arid coastal scrublands as low as six hundred feet above sea level; others range over higher plains; and some occupy—or perhaps have retreated to—slopes at or above the snow line, nearly fourteen hundred feet in elevation.

Adults generally weigh between 175 and three hundred pounds, though a few have been known to grow larger. With all paws on the ground, a typical adult is less than three feet high at the shoulders, but standing upright it may be as tall as a man, sometimes taller.

In Ecuador, the bears feed largely on pambili palms, climbing to tear off foliage, then descending to eat the fallen fronds. In Venezuela's highlands, they eat the leaf bases and inner parts of

The spectacled, or Andean, bear is the sole survivor of a subfamily known as short-faced bears that once roamed North and South America. Seen almost in profile, the muzzle is obviously much shorter and blunter than that of other bears.

Resting next to a mossy, rotting log, this spectacled bear may be taking a respite from hunting insects, lizards, or other small prey, but the species is more herbivorous than most bears. It eats ground vegetation and also climbs trees to feed on leaves, branches, and fruit.

the puya, which looks rather like a giant pineapple top. Indeed, they browse on many plants so tough that few other animals can chew them. Foods include palm nuts and leaves, cactus, fruits, honey (when they can find it), and corn or sugarcane, where man or nature provides it. When or where preferred vegetation is scarce, they prey on insects, birds, small mammals, and reptiles, and on rare occasions may kill a llama. Reported prey includes deer, vicunas, and guanacos. Like bears elsewhere, a few slaughter livestock and are in turn killed by ranchers or farmers.

Spectacled bears often build stick mats high in trees; these rough nests are daytime beds, which most other bears make on the ground. South American bears spend long periods high in trees, alternately resting and climbing nimbly to feed. Although reputed to be ferocious (like any bear when motivated), they seem to be somewhat more timid than North American black bears, and when on the ground they generally avoid human intrusion.

Temperatures in the Andean highlands can drop low, but not low enough to induce winter denning. Females den shortly before giving birth, whereas males seldom if ever den. Mating takes place from April through June as a rule, but the breeding period is longer and less well defined than in species of colder climates. Both the mating and gestation period appear to be unusually variable. Throughout most of the range, births occur from November through February, usually about six weeks before the peak of the fruit season in a given locale. Since pregnancy may last more than eight months or under six, the spectacled bear enjoys the advantage of delayed implantation, just as northern species do. Thus the female's energy-costing stage of pregnancy coincides with the fruit season.

Birth weights range up to a pound or more, which is heavier than for most species. This probably reflects the conditions of the life cycle, since denning is short and the young soon must move about. The den tends to be a mere rudimentary nest under tree roots or rocks. Cubs number one, two, or rarely, three.

Like other bears, mother and cubs communicate vocally and by actions and postures that constitute body language. Nursing cubs make a purring sound. When disturbed, the sow and cubs maintain contact with high trills, and there is a screeching alarm call. An alarmed cub may scramble onto its mother's back and ride the mother as it flees. It has also been reliably reported that a mother sometimes scoops up a cub with one paw and holds it against its chest while running on three legs.

Adult males have been observed with females and cubs, though spectacled bears do not remain paired after mating. Since a male bear of any species may prey on cubs, a mother seldom tolerates a male's presence. Reports of contented family foraging invite skepticism, but unusual environmental conditions may nurture unusual responses or adaptations. The verdict awaits future field studies.

Easier to accept is the fact that in years of poor forage a pregnant spectacled bear may reabsorb its embryos, undergoing a natural abortion. This occurs in many mammals, including animals as different as deer. Cubs born in such circumstances might die, or the mother might die, which would doom them as well. Thus nature provides a means of survival in lean times and a chance to procreate again when conditions improve.

As often as not, the facial markings on a spectacled bear are intermittent or end above the eyes, the result barely resembling spectacles. The highly variable markings frequently extend down along the cheeks and may join under the chin or on the upper chest to form a patchy blaze.

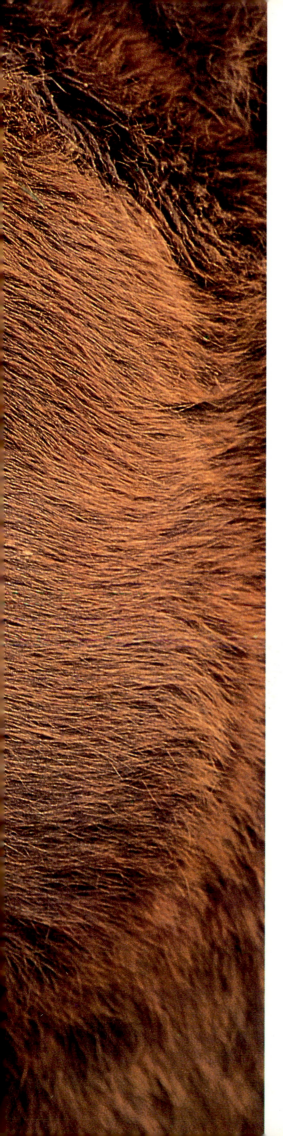

4.
THE MAGNIFICENT BROWN BEAR

The Alaskan brown bears of Kodiak Island and its vicinity vie with polar bears as the world's largest carnivorous mammals. There are larger whales, but of all land-based animals only the elephant, rhinoceros, and hippopotamus attain more prodigious size. There is some circumstantial evidence that another subspecies of the brown bear, a rare and little-known denizen of Siberia's Kamchatka Peninsula, may actually grow even larger and heavier than the Kodiak bears, but that supposition is based only on a few tracks and one gigantic bear skin and therefore remains to be proven! Unless they have interbred with the smaller, inland grizzlies, male Alaskan brown bears—or coastal grizzlies, as they are also known—attain a weight between eight hundred and twelve hundred pounds at eight or nine years of age. But one Kodiak brown was reported to weigh 1,656 pounds. The skull of another measured very nearly thirteen inches wide and a hair less than eighteen inches long! The hind feet of such a bear can leave tracks ten inches wide and almost seventeen inches from claws to heel.

When an eight-hundred-pound brown bear is driven by hunger, anger, or mere determination, it exhibits a strength that impresses observers as power incarnate. A bear was seen lying on an Alaska beach next to the carcass of a large sea lion. The observer could not tell whether the sea lion had been washed ashore dead or had ventured close to shore and been killed by the bear, but he could see that it was a big one, perhaps nearly double the weight of that particular bear. The breeze shifted and the bear caught the scent of the observer, who was in a skiff. Rising slowly, almost casually, the bear waded into the water for a closer view of the boat, stared for a moment, growled, returned to the carcass, and with its jaws got a firm grip on the sea lion's neck. It then proceeded to walk backwards, dragging its enormously heavy prize fifty yards up a steep beach, over sizable logs, and into the woods. On another occasion a brown bear was caught by researchers in a snare and vented its frustration by snapping a small tree in two with a single bite and then chewing through several larger ones.

*Although the cocoa color of this Alaskan grizzly is
not uncommon among the inland population,
one of the animal's immediate ancestors may well
have been a coastal brown bear.*

These brown bears exhibit the color variations seen to some extent in coastal populations and more commonly in the North American interior. The setting is Alaska, and the paler animal has the color often described in the literature as blond.

Having satisfied itself that nothing is amiss, this erect grizzly has finished scanning the distance and is already looking down at what the ground has to offer. In an instant the animal will drop to all fours.

These Alaskan brown bears were photographed at McNeil River, where great numbers of them congregate during the salmon run. The two bears challenging each other are disputing a choice fishing spot. Fights sometimes become ferocious, but more often a dominant male (or female with yearling cubs) bluffs a slightly smaller, younger rival into withdrawing. The bear devouring the salmon is not standing on its hind legs in a deep pool but sitting comfortably on its haunches. After satisfying its initial hunger, it may carry its catches ashore to eat them.

Since the northern summer is short and the winter long, coastal brown bears ravenously devour the bounty provided by their Alaskan environment during summer's peak. Roaming the tidal flats, they graze heavily on sedge grass, which has a very high protein content, and also eat a wide array of other vegetation and any flesh they can find. Soon the run of spawning salmon begins, and they feed on the fish with equal or greater voracity. In summer, one of these bears may consume more than eighty pounds of food in a day, thereby gaining three to six pounds of fat in a period of twenty-four hours.

Brown bears are quick to anger when provoked by any creature, including their own kind, and havoc would seem inevitable on the salmon streams, but this is not the case. A renowned congregation site lies some 140 miles north of Kodiak on the McNeil River. Here the river rumbles over a series of low falls. When the salmon reach this point, they rest briefly and then struggle and leap their way up the falls and shallow rapids. New arrivals swell the numbers of salmon, and the bears gather to catch them. This place has been made a sanctuary, with resident biologists serving as guides and supervisors—not only interpreting but guarding against bear-human

A rock amid rapids makes an excellent feeding station. The force of the current here may be powerful enough to knock a man over and shoot him downriver, but the bears plow through it with no evident labor.

Contrary to a widespread notion, bears seldom attempt to flip a salmon out of the water, a technique that would fail too often. Many of them swiftly extend one leg and pin a salmon to the bottom. This bear will anchor a salmon with the left paw and then clutch the fish in its mouth.

At the height of a spawning run, bears become sufficiently sated to be selective, even fussy, eating only favorite parts of the fish, such as the head and skin. Here a bear strips away what it wants and may leave the remainder for gulls, foxes, and the like.

conflicts—for up to ten visitors at a time, each with a four-day permit. These are without doubt the world's most closely and constantly observed wild bears, and their strategies for preventing mayhem among themselves are well documented.

Fights occur, but not often, and most of them involve more bluff than blood—a matter of one animal's testing another's dominance and self-confidence. As the bears arrive, a definite hierarchy takes form. Generally, large males in their prime years are the alpha, or top-ranking, bears. They move directly to the best fishing spots and defend them if challenged. Should a competitor approach too closely, the dominant bear may have to do no more than stare it down. If that does not spur retreat, stronger body or facial language usually will: baring or clicking the teeth, snarling or making a chomping sound, popping the mouth open and shut quickly and repeatedly while salivating, or merely lowering the head. There is an old, evidently valid belief among Indians and Aleuts that a bear moving slowly with its head lower than the hump of its shoulder is a bear to be avoided. Some dominant boar bears return to the same favorite fishing spot year after year and tolerate no rivals close to it.

The animal in the forward position is the mother, and the slightly smaller one is her cub, playing or showing affection. Even large yearling brown bears stay close to their mothers in case of trouble on the river. If she is challenged, they usually flank her or hang back slightly and mimic her threat display.

An inexperienced bear reaches prematurely for a sockeye salmon leaping up a typical Alaskan falls. By trial and error amounting to experimentation, it will learn to anchor fish against the rocks with a paw or, less frequently, grab them with its mouth as they top the falls.

In the second rank of dominance are sow bears accompanied by yearlings. Females with younger cubs are aggressive and dangerous but less able to cope with rivals. A new mother must keep watch on its cubs to make sure one of them does not stray far enough to be attacked by an adult. The mother must place itself between them and an adversary. Moreover, their small size and timid helplessness when an aggressor approaches may invite escalated aggression. Yearlings, on the other hand, have learned how to behave, and they tend to imitate the mother in action and attitude, as if ready to fight at her side if the family is bullied.

Next in order of dominance are the smaller, younger males and still smaller females. These

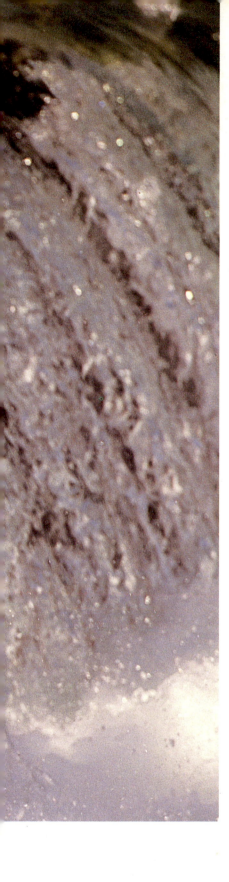

Poised on the lip of a low falls in Katmai National Park, a bear uses the snapping technique to capture salmon struggling to top the rise. Bears exhibit very individualistic styles and methods of fishing.

animals seem to accept their subordinate status calmly, at least for the time being. Still they manage to get their share of salmon, and occasionally one of them gets lucky when a big male has eaten its fill and suddenly becomes tolerant. Trouble comes when a previously subordinate male feels capable of ousting a dominant male and has grown big and strong enough to defy threats. The ensuing fight may be perfunctory or fierce, and blows may be inflicted that would kill lesser animals, but an experienced McNeil River biologist has stated that never once has he seen a conflict result in serious crippling.

The bears' methods of catching fish are intriguing and more efficient than they appear. The popular misconception that a bear normally bats salmon out of a stream must be based on the fact that some young, inexperienced bears do this and occasionally succeed, but not with any regularity. Another popular notion is that bears almost always use their mouths to capture prey, catching leaping salmon in midair. This generally happens when a bear takes a station on the lip of a falls and seizes them as they writhe and flip their way toward waiting jaws. Actually, there seems to be great variation and individuality in the techniques used. Many bears stand or stalk in very shallow riffles and pin passing salmon with one or both paws, then use their teeth to grab the quarry. This probably the most efficient approach. Some bears do use their mouths to capture fish underwater or

Standing to get a clear view, this grizzly has an alertly interested, almost questioning expression in its eyes, facial position, and slightly open mouth. Bears appear to be much more expressive than most animals.

writhing on the surface, and more than one has been seen wading across a deep pool with its head underwater, snatching salmon with its teeth.

America's inland grizzlies were originally regarded as a separate species since they are larger than most European browns, smaller than Alaska's coastal browns, and distinctive in color—most often having a silver-tipped or lightly frosted coat of guard hairs over the tan or brown. Hence they look somewhat grayish, or grizzly. Like all browns, they have a pronounced muscle mass above the shoulder blades, forming a hump behind the base of the neck in contrast to the smoothly rounded backs of other species. Still, they were not recognized as browns, and they received their own scientific designation, which reflected their vicious reputation: *Ursus horribilis*, literally "horrible," or terrifying, bear. Even among scientists there was some dispute before they were relegated to their proper subspecific rank, *U. arctos horribilis*.

A very young cub rides its mother's back. The mothers tend to be rather permissive, except in matters of safety, and often allow the cubs to scramble all over them. But a cub that disobeys, straying too far or refusing to come when called, may be cuffed hard enough to make it bawl.

A sow brown bear stands up to survey the surroundings for intruders as her cubs graze and explore—but never dare move as far from a mother's protection as black bear cubs would.

The Alaskan brown bear was likewise misperceived as a distinct species for many years—after all, a mature male may be over four feet high at the shoulder when down on all fours, measure twice that in head-and-body length, rise upright to tower ten feet tall, have double the weight of a grizzly, and more than double the weight of a European brown. All the same, it is now positively understood to be a subspecies (*U. a. middendorffi*), essentially a grizzly grown huge on an unusually rich diet and blessed with the genes of oversized ancestors. It is worth noting here that in some areas coastal browns and interior grizzlies meet (while black bears give them a wide berth) and interbreed, resulting in an intergradation of size and color.

Furthermore, size and color are variable in both races, Characteristically, the coastal browns are, indeed, some shade of brown or tan, while grizzlies may be true silvertips, but in some regions they may be almost as black as an Eastern black bear—though never as glossy—or they may be the color of chocolate, copper, or bronze. Many of the Toklat grizzlies around Mount McKinley are almost blond. Subspecies in other parts of the world are predominantly brown, although in Europe alone the color ranges from dark brown to russet or copper, and a couple of more pronounced variations occur in Asia.

No real doubt remains that all of the world's races are of a single species, probably having

Two cubs are the most common number, both for interior grizzlies and coastal browns such as these. In food-rich locales of easy living, however, triplets like those seen here are not at all uncommon.

spread westward from Asia through Europe and even, at one time, gained a northern African foothold in Tunisia and Algeria, while also spreading eastward and crossing the isthmus that once joined Alaska to Siberia. For many years, taxonomists were divided into two schools, the consolidators and the "splitters." The latter group tended to grant species status on the basis of minor anatomical or physiological differences. Eventually the consolidators proved their case, yet vestiges of the splitter opposition remain in reference works that allude to more than fifty subspecies of brown bear in Europe, Asia, and North America. At least some of those divisions must surely be more specious than valid, despite color, size, and geographic considerations. In accordance with the trend toward manageable consolidation, most taxonomists now enumerate fewer than a dozen subspecies.

For the most part, it would be meaningless as well as tedious to describe all the minor variations here, whether ten or fifty plus, but a few are sufficiently intriguing to merit attention.

In parts of the Himalayas, including northern India, lives a bear similar to the American grizzly except for color. A reddish brown bear with white tipping that gives it a frosted or grizzled tinge, this race is known as the red bear, or isabelline bear (*U. a. isabellinus*). In the wild, it probably subsists chiefly on vegetation and occasional small prey plus carrion. Occasionally, animals such as ibex and other high-country dwellers are killed in avalanches, providing a sizable sup-

Hot but not uncomfortable, a grizzly lies supine on a summer day. If the animal does become overheated, it will probably seek water or make its way to higher, windier ground.

On Kodiak Island, the locale where Alaskan brown bears grow biggest, this salivating brown is licking at a tree crevice that probably holds insects.

This young grizzly is trying mightily to reach an eagles' nest. One of the parent birds is in the nest and will put up a fierce fight when the bear comes close, but may not prevent the marauder from taking eggs or nestlings. In another year, this bear probably will no longer be able to climb trees.

Curiosity or hunger prompted this brown bear cub to investigate a porcupine. Unfortunately, porcupine quills are barbed and tend to work their way inward rather than out. The wounds may fester, and if the quills prevent normal eating, the cub may be doomed.

Still wet after a fishing session, these bears at McNeil River Sanctuary are a temporarily bonded pair during mating season, and they have wandered away from the water to copulate.

plement. In the introductory section of this book, I mentioned that the sloth bear—a species regarded as very dangerous—has been trained to dance by street entertainers in India. I have also read that Himalayan peasants shoot red bears that are accompanied by cubs, then sell the cubs to itinerant entertainers for use as dancing bears. It is safe to assume that a typical red bear is as dangerous as a big grizzly, but it is also true that brown bears of all races are extremely intelligent and therefore prized by animal trainers.

A subspecies found in Tibet and neighboring provinces of China is known as the horse bear (*U. a. pruinosus*) because it frequently has a pale or whitish saddle marking across its shoulders. A greatly feared animal, it is reported to be a confirmed killer of people. In this region, ground is being cleared and croplands expanded, which brings the farmers into contact—and conflict—with bears that will not tolerate intrusion. At present, farmers are being killed, but it seems inevitable that ultimately the bears will be forced into more remote mountain fastnesses, just as the plains grizzlies were in America.

Mention has been made of the giant brown bears of Siberia's Kamchatka Peninsula, which

At Alaska's McNeil River, famous for its gatherings of fishing bears, a contented bear crunches a salmon while an entourage of gulls awaits the scraps. The birds are tolerated most of the time, but will be rushed and temporarily scattered if they get underfoot.

Having emerged from its winter den while snow still blankets the ground, this bear has already started to shed its winter coat. It may speed the process as it relieves itching by rubbing against trees.

This tree in the Yukon has been scarred by a grizzly's claws. Both grizzlies and black bears stand erect and stretch upward to scratch tree trunks, but grizzlies reach much higher.

This tree has not merely been scratched by a grizzly but stripped of a large section of bark. Bears can ravage trees by claw-marking them, and can kill prized timber by girdling the trunks to eat the cambium.

The Alaskan brown bear—long thought to be a distinct species differing anatomically and genetically from European and Asian brown bears and the American grizzly—is now sometimes called the coastal grizzly. However, all of those bears are now known to be the same species. An Alaskan brown like this one grows to enormous proportions chiefly because its habitat provides an unusually rich diet.

The enormous tracks of a brown bear sink deep into the dense muck of a tidal flat. Their size and the great length of their claw indentations make them easy to distinguish from a black bear's prints. Where both species are prevalent, black bears are apt to avoid browns.

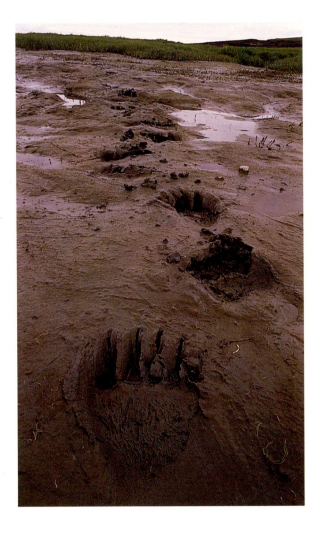

Serenely majestic in the twilight of late summer, this animal typifies the brown bears of the Alaskan Peninsula, and no creature is more beautiful.

The behavior of this European brown bear—standing to investigate a sight, sound, or smell—mirrors that of some American and Asian subspecies.

Like other young bears, these European bears bite gently as they enjoy a play fight. All the same, they instinctively go for each other's necks, just as they would in a serious fight or in attacking sizable prey—including livestock.

A European brown bear sits up, clutching its hind feet with its forepaws. Bears quite often hold their hind feet in this manner while sitting upright or lying on their backs.

Youngsters often watch from a streambank as their elders, wading or standing in water too deep and often too swift for them, catch passing salmon.

Engaged in a mock fight, these European brown bears will probably tire of the game quickly and move apart to feed. However, if one of the bears becomes too rough, the play may turn into furious combat.

appear merely to be a local strain of *U. a. beringianus*, the Siberian brown bear, and—except for size—not very different from that prototype or from the Manchurian variety, *U. a. manchuricus*. The Kamchatka bears are said to reach a weight of eighteen hundred pounds, but no reliable observer has yet seen one. The estimate is merely based on tracks, a single enormous hide, and descriptions given by natives. Future field research may determine the truth. A bear of that size would overshadow the largest Kodiak brown or polar bear.

Japan has an undetermined number of Asian black bears and about three thousand brown bears (*U. a. higuma*), close kin of the Manchurian brown bears. All of the Japanese brown bears live on Hokkaido, the northernmost island, where, unfortunately, they come into frequent conflict with farmers and fishermen.

Field research on brown bears, including the use of radio collars to track the animals' move-

The several bears seen here will not challenge one another, as their chosen fishing stations are far enough apart so that no animal will feel crowded or threatened. There are, of course, salmon enough for all.

These are Manchurian brown bears, one of several Asian subspecies. Some reference works allude to more than fifty European, Asian, and American subspecies, but most taxonomists have consolidated these geographic races into about ten classifications.

Young bears at McNeil River seem to be fighting but are merely playing. This may be instinctive practice in preparation for the assumption of dominant status when they grow big enough to challenge a mature bear for the best fishing spot.

This grizzly has managed to kill a caribou and is resting near it after eating its fill. The bear will not leave the kill before devouring a great deal more.

Raising dust, a bear dislodges loose earth and stones as it walks, skids, and slides down a steep slope.

ments and activities, has been more common and intense in North America than in Asia or Europe. Accounts of their breeding and denning habits are largely based on American bear populations, but it is reasonable to assume that other bears have similar characteristics, with minor variations depending on latitude and local topography and habitat.

A young bear futilely chases a fish. Failures will far outnumber successes at first, but the animal will learn from experience, gradually becoming adept and developing its own fishing style with paws or jaws.

A bit inland from the Alaskan coast, brown bears and interior grizzlies interbreed, producing the common intergraded coloration shown here. This bear is probably smaller than its brown parent and bigger than its grizzly parent.

The enormous pads of a brown bear's foot are stable platforms and formidable weapons. The long claws are relatively straight, not well formed for climbing after the bear is nearly full grown, but perfect for prodigious digging.

Panting and with its tongue lolling, a grizzly cools itself after the exertion of foraging on a hot day. Grizzlies are much better adapted to cold than to heat. At one time they were common as far south as Mexico but kept to the high plateaus and mountains, whereas farther north they were also found on the plains.

Where few tall, thick trees are available for rubbing, a grizzly will make do with a sapling. This bear is rubbing its head, probably scent-marking the tree rather than relieving an itch.

A mother brown bear leads three large cubs along a well-worn trail to an Alaskan creek. Triplets are more common in the coastal habitat of southeastern Alaska than elsewhere, probably because an unusually rich diet keeps the animals in optimal condition.

A young grizzly walks onto a beaver dam. The bear may only be using the dam as a walkway, but the scent of beavers will not go undetected, and any beaver that dares to investigate the disturbance will be very unfortunate.

Two bears plod through Alaska's Denali National Park on a sunny day. With snow covering the ground and no green sprouts to graze, they may dig into a hillside to excavate sleeping marmots.

An arctic ground squirrel flees down a snowy hillside in panic with a sow grizzly in pursuit. The little rodent has already escaped without knowing it. The bear's initial lunge has failed, and it cannot catch the prey.

This grizzly is not in the water to catch fish. The animal is merely enjoying a bath. If it detected a fish moving nearby, however, it would instantly take a hungry interest.

A young European brown bear laps water from a stream. Bears need plenty of water and frequently come to ponds or streams to drink in the evening.

Ten-day-old cubs, their eyes and ears not yet quite open, nestle against their mother in the den. Incessantly hungry, they will soon grow restless and seek a nipple. The grayish infant coat is typical of grizzlies and begins to brown at this age.

A female brown bear in Europe lies on its back as its two cubs prepare to nurse.

A brown bear cub peers at
the photographer,
although its mother
already seems to have lost
interest. A cub will often
nuzzle its mother's back,
probably to gain a
sensation of security.

On a grassy flat near a
tidal creek, a young bear
investigates a long-dead
tree limb, probably
driftwood, in case it
harbors insects or other
edible morsels.

5.
SUN, MOON, AND SLOTH— ASIA'S UNIQUE TRIO

The Sun Bear

The world's smallest bear—not much bigger than a large dog—inhabits tropical and subtropical regions of southern and southeastern Asia and nearby islands. Although Europeans and Americans generally assume that bears are distributed only from the temperate zone north into the arctic, Asia's sun bear and sloth bear are found near and even below the equator, as is the South American spectacled bear. The sun bear is essentially a jungle animal, occurring in the forests of Burma and Thailand, possibly in adjacent regions of Laos, Cambodia, and Vietnam, and southward through the Malay Peninsula and the islands of Borneo, Sumatra, and Java. In the 1980s it was also rediscovered west of Burma, in India, where it had been considered extinct. It resides, among other places, in a tiger preserve in India, where it is probably safe from further decline.

Long a victim of increased farming, timbering, and illegal hunting, the sun bear, also known as the Malayan bear, has been listed as an endangered species since the 1970s. To curtail trade in bear paws and gall bladders—used throughout the Orient in soups, tonics, folk medicines, and aphrodisiacs—the monitoring branch of the World Wildlife Fund opened additional offices in Malaysia in 1991 and began training additional field investigators. Naturalist and author Terry Domico traveled to Sabah (North Borneo) to assess the situation, and during his stay found only nine bears, all in captivity. These, of course, included pets, although this is illegal.

From tip of nose to rump, this diminutive bear is seldom more than about four and a half feet long. A couple of decades ago, authorities alluded to two-hundred-pound specimens, but the figure may well have been erroneous. The animal, after all, stands only about two feet high at the shoulder when all its feet are on the ground. Weights from sixty to slightly more than 140 pounds are more or less normal for adults, and a mature sun bear in the wild is considered big if it exceeds 110 pounds. It has short, dense black fur and commonly, but not always, a pale or yel-

Relaxing on its back, this sun bear exudes contentment in its lush, tropical surroundings. But its future is hardly secure. Largely owing to deforestation and poaching, this species is endangered.

The marking on this sun bear is a broad, almost circular patch that is speckled with a large disk of black in the center. There is no such variation in more important characteristics, such as the long, curved claws for climbing and digging.

In Asian folklore, a yellow crescent symbolizes the rising sun, and the sun bear's name is derived from the marking on its neck and upper chest. However, this marking is quite variable in shape and is not even present on some individuals.

A sun bear clutches a branched stem in its paw and nibbles the leaves and buds. The species eats a wide assortment of vegetation, both on the ground and in trees.

lowish crescent on its chest. The name sun bear is probably derived from this marking, for in Eastern folklore a yellow crescent represents the rising sun, though to Western eyes it more closely resembles a crescent moon. Even when present, the marking is quite valuable; it may be an irregular patch, a bib, a necklace, or a thick circle with a black center.

The shaded floor of a tropical forest has relatively little vegetation, but sun bears are opportunists that can find a wide variety of foods, hunting swiftly on the ground and climbing with great agility and ease. In fact, they spend many daylight hours in trees, resting in crude nests constructed of branches and twigs. Their diet includes small rodents, lizards, birds, earthworms, and all the insects they can find.

The sun bear has a long, extensible tongue that it uses to lick up any exposed insects it finds and to extract termites, ants, and bee grubs from their nests.

Every variety of bear seems to enjoy sitting on its haunches. This may be a particularly comfortable position for an animal with short legs and a chunky anatomical structure.

A mother bear stands guard over a cub and grooms it as it sprawls at the base of a tree. Unfortunately, the animals damage coconut palms, earning the enmity of plantation owners.

The Moon Bear

The more northerly habitat of the Asian black bear, or moon bear, is in sharp contrast to that of the sun bear. Also called the Tibetan or Himalayan black bear, it is found in Iran, Afghanistan, northern Pakistan, across the Tibetan Plateau, in Manchuria and other well forested portions of China, on Taiwan and the Japanese islands, and as far south as Bangladesh and Laos.

The name moon bear refers to a white or ivory chest marking, usually a crescent or chevron that is common but occasionally narrow, faint, or absent. The chin is also white or whitish, and the muzzle is usually brown or tan. The remainder of the coat is black, and is so long on the neck and shoulders that it forms a thick ruff, almost like a sideward-flaring mane. The large, round ears are set wide apart on the head, which is also rounded. Many of the bears in the southern part of the range have shorter, thinner coats, with less of the dense undercoating, than those found at higher elevations or in the north. The claws are short, strong, and deeply curved, very useful in climbing trees, yet the larger adults, particularly males, lose some of their climbing ability and keep to the ground for the most part.

This animal is built rather like the American black bear, but is somewhat smaller. Although a big male may weigh four hundred pounds or more, the average is two hundred to two hundred and fifty pounds or so, with females slightly smaller than males. When the Asian black bear stands on its hind legs, any superficial resemblance to the American black bear vanishes because of the very distinctive ears and the wide ruff, flaring to the sides like a wind-blown hooded cape. And this bear stands upright often, being the most bipedal of all bears. It has been known to walk a quarter mile on its hind legs, and circus bears in China and other parts of Asia have been trained to walk a double slackrope. (A slackrope is allowed to sag somewhat, unlike a tightrope, and two such ropes are strung parallel a few feet above the ground. The bear steps onto them from a platform, placing one hind foot on each rope, and slowly walks their length.) Some of these bears are active during the day, but typically in most parts of their range they spend the daylight hours dozing in a cave, hollow tree, or other natural shelter and emerge at dusk to begin

This is an Asian black bear of the Himalayas. Predictably, the species tends to be larger and have a thicker coat in the northern part of its range than in the warmer southern regions.

An Asian black, or moon, bear swims a stream. The name Himalayan black bear is sometimes used but is rather misleading, because the animal's range extends all the way from the Himalayas to Laos and Taiwan.

feeding. They eat nuts, fruits, leaves, buds, and other vegetation, both in trees and on the ground. Like other bears, they also feed on insects, carrion, and any small animals they can catch. Unfortunately, they also prey on larger animals, often killing domestic livestock in some areas. In Indochina they approach villages to feed on grain in the fields. And in some regions they earn even greater hatred among the local human population by damaging trees. In oak, beech, cherry, and dogwood trees, all of which provide food, they often build basking nests, breaking off branches to do so. In addition to eating buds, leaves, fruits, and nuts, they strip the bark from some trees to reach the cambium. In Japan the most valuable timber species, cedars and cypress, seem to suffer most, and as many as three thousand bears are killed annually, both as nuisances and for sport.

Asian black bears are also slain because they are feared. They have a reputation for ferocity. Although some authorities have suggested that the reputation is exaggerated, the fact is that in Japan alone two or three people are killed and up to a score injured by the bears every year. These animals are short-tempered not only when guarding cubs or a food source but when roused from their winter torpor. When an American black bear is disturbed in its den, more often than not it awakens slowly, reluctantly, and is groggy enough to allow an intruder to retreat. Asian black bears are more likely to awaken quickly and in a rage. Several years ago, when a team of researchers and students very cautiously approached a den, an enormous male bear came out and attacked. One of the students probably would have been killed had not Terry Domico blasted the animal with a repellent spray.

Preferred denning sites are hollow logs and trees, though caves or similar shelters are sometimes used. In the southern part of the range, the bears can forage during most of the winter and may sleep for only short periods. Farther north, they den from November through March or early April.

As with the sun bear, courtship is brief, perhaps just a day or two in May sufficing. But the mating period is regionally variable and long, with mating observed in March and also as late as December. Indian moon bears are reported to mate in autumn. Two or sometimes three cubs, weighing about eight ounces, are born in seven or eight months. Their eyes open quickly, only about a week after birth, and after a month or so they follow their mother about. They remain with their mother for a year or two, or longer in a few instances. It is possible—though sharply contrasting with the behavior of other bears—that this species may once in a great while allow cubs to remain through the next breeding cycle, for moon bears have been seen with two sets of cubs. Still, it seems at least as likely that these are cases of orphan adoption.

The Asian black bear has a broad, full, manelike ruff and very round, wideset ears. Most often there is a white or ivory crescent on the chest. Its other common name, moon bear, refers to this marking.

The Sloth Bear

English big-game hunters shipped bear skins home from India in the eighteenth century, along with fanciful descriptions of the animals hanging upside down from jungle trees and having trunklike snouts. But for chance, the species might just as easily have been named the elephant bear. However, a curator at the British Museum, misguided by the descriptions and by the animal's long, deeply curved claws, admirably shaped for gripping, classified it as a "bear sloth"—a sloth with bearish characteristics. Then, in 1810, a live specimen arrived in Paris, home of the great anatomist Georges Cuvier and a center of studies in the natural sciences. Cuvier's erudition was not needed in this case; even a layman could see that it was a bear. It was reclassified and the name reversed to sloth bear. So it has been known ever since, although it is also, and more appropriately, called the Indian bear.

It is found from the base of the Himalayas southward in forested areas to the tip of India and the island of Sri Lanka (Ceylon), as far eastward as Assam, and in Nepal's Chitwan National Park. Total numbers are probably between seven thousand and ten thousand. I have learned to my chagrin that the animal was common in India when I was there and, indeed, as recently as two decades ago. Deforestation has caused a severe decrease in its population. It is adaptable to a rather wide variety of woods habitat, from the northern thorn forests to the humid, tropical jungles of the south, but to thrive in the wild it must have forest of some type.

The confusion it bought to the British Museum two centuries ago is understandable, for it has to be the most unbearish bear of all. Typically, it has a long, shaggy, rumpled coat of black, occasionally with glints of russet. The hair between the shoulders and on the back of the neck forms a wide and ragged ruff. Usually the chest is marked by a white or rusty white chevron, sometimes

These sloth bears—a mother and nearly grown offspring— are playing, not fighting. If their mouths look partially toothless, so they are. They lack front teeth, and the mouth is remarkably constructed not for cutting flesh but for sucking termites out of their nests.

The sloth bear of India is a shaggy beast quite unlike other bears. Neither is it anything like a sloth. It owes its common name to scientific misconceptions in the late eighteenth century.

Its snout garlanded by a sprig of vegetation, this sloth bear looks gentle and playful. Appearances notwithstanding, they are feared by villagers in many areas. Their reputation may be exaggerated, as they tend to make bluff charges, terminating in a roaring upright display.

narrow, sometimes wide, sometimes U- or V-shaped. The muzzle is indeed long and somewhat tubular—though not trunklike—and is whitish or gray and sparsely haired. It has extremely flexible, protrusile lips, nostrils it can close at will to keep insects out, a long tongue, a hollowed bony palate, and to complete the unbearish picture, no front teeth.

An especially favored food is honey (as with all bears where honey is available). They also feed on ants and other insects, berries and other fruits, carrion, and probably an occasional small mammal, amphibian, or reptile. They are fond of mohwa flowers, which bloom in the spring in India and are fermented by villagers to make a beverage. The presence of mohwa trees therefore causes competition and sometimes conflict between bears and humans, as does the bears' inclination to feed on cultivated sugarcane, corn, and yams. Sloth bears are chiefly nocturnal, but are sometimes active at any time of day. Excellent climbers, they forage both in trees and on the ground. Like other Asian bears, they have a reputation for unpredictable viciousness, but they are not nearly as aggressive as some other bear species. Trouble ensues when a human blunders close to a sloth bear that is ambling about slowly, preoccupied with foraging, and is abruptly alarmed. The bear's typical reaction, in Domico's words, "is a spectacular bluff charge terminating in a roaring, upright display. But sometimes the encounter may turn into a tragic mauling before the panicked bear rushes off."

These bears are extremely vocal and more gregarious than other species. They apparently communicate with one another via facial expressions, body language, and a large array of howls, squeals, roars, yelps, and even humming. Asian bears, including this one, have been observed to suck a paw and hum on occasion while at rest. This is probably a reflexive action, a vestigial habit of nursing, as in human thumbsucking.

Male bears sometimes scrape tree trunks and rub the trunks with their flanks—as do other bears in woodlands. Since bears are not as territorial as some other carnivores, this is probably a marking behavior to attract mates. Mating is noisy, and courtship, though brief, is marked by play-fighting and hugging. Spring is mating season in much of India, but in Sri Lanka breeding has been observed at all times of year. There is no denning or pronounced seasonal dormancy, but the two or sometimes three cubs are born most often in a cave or temporary den dug under a boulder or jumble of rocks. The gestation period is six to seven months. The cubs are about the size of newborn American black bears or perhaps a trifle smaller, and the adults are about the size of a small American black bear, no more than about three feet high at the shoulder when standing on all four feet, and perhaps six feet in length. Females are much smaller than males; the latter may weigh as much as three hundred pounds.

This young sloth bear cub is examining a log for insects or honey. The cub's muzzle will grow much longer in proportion to its face as well as more tubular, an adaptation for "vacuum feeding."

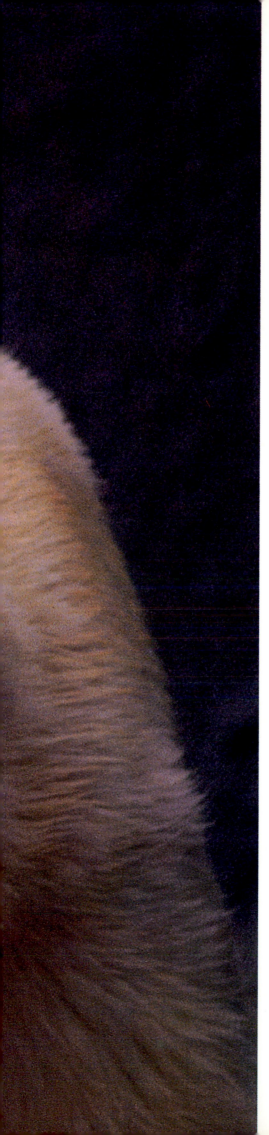

6.

POLAR BEARS—NAVIGATORS OF THE NORTHERN ICE

Through photographs, documentary films, articles in the popular press, and zoo specimens, the image of the polar bear has become almost universally familiar, and exhaustive field studies have been in progress for some time, yet the great bear of the arctic is surrounded by at least as much mystery and speculation as any of the other ursine species. Eskimo hunt Nanook—their name for the animal—but they also revere it, attributing incredible intelligence and supernatural powers to the ice bear, or snow bear, as *Ursus maritimus* is also widely known. Much has been learned since 1922, when Robert Flaherty produced his pioneering and classic documentary film *Nanook of the North*, a study of the daily life of both Eskimo and bear, but much still remains to be learned.

Authorities have concluded that polar bears evolved from Siberian brown bears between 250,000 and 100,000 years ago, during the Pleistocene, or glacial, epoch. Recently, however, some scientists have accorded a slightly greater age to the species in its present form, about 260,000 years. As early as that perhaps, the bear had acquired its several unique characteristics in addition to color—or lack thereof. All bears have a somewhat bowlegged, pigeon-toed walk, which evidently provides traction, but it is more pronounced in the polar bear. The feet, especially the hind feet, are somewhat more rounded than those of the brown bear—broader for their length. Moreover, the soles of the feet are haired, whereas those of other bears are naked. The hair provides insulation and, probably more important, traction that prevents rearward slipping when the animal traverses or climbs up slippery ice floes.

Since seals are the polar bear's primary prey, an analogy to the seal's coat is appropriate. Its rearward-oriented grain helps a seal climb out of water onto slick ice. Early cross-country skiers borrowed this principle by hooking a sealskin strip to the bottom of each ski. When sliding forward on level or downhill snow, the fur lay back flat to form a smooth surface; when pointed uphill, the moment the skis began to slide back the fur caught at the snow, preventing slippage.

When a polar bear's coat is unstained, its color varies from snow white to ivory. The beauty of its coat is matched by functional efficiency. It serves as camouflage when bears stalk seals, and the individual hairs are actually clear, hollow heat conductors as well as insulators. They trap solar heat and transfer it down to the black skin underneath.

The furry soles of a polar bear's feet work the same way even on ice or crusted snow, and on soft snow the broadness of the feet spreads the animal's weight, rather like snowshoes.

Moreover, the toes of the forepaws are partially webbed for swimming, a characteristic shared with very few other mammals. The broadness of the feet surely helps in this respect, too. Indeed, polar bears are astonishing swimmers. When hunting or merely playing, they can leap out of the water in the manner of porpoises and seals; they can tread water and float; and at an average speed of about six miles an hour they can swim sixty miles or perhaps farther without resting. The forefeet rhythmically paddle, while the hind feet are used chiefly as rudders. Their underwater eyesight is excellent, allowing them to catch prey beneath the surface. Brown bears sometimes hold their breath and submerge themselves for brief periods to catch salmon underwater, but their ability is no match for that of the polar bear, which closes its nostrils, flattens its ears, and may remain submerged for as long as two minutes.

Swimming is one of the polar bear's methods of hunting seals, but it has also been known to snatch an occasional shellfish from the bottom in shallow water and to come up under unsuspecting seabirds resting on the surface. A sixty-mile swim means at least ten hours in the water, all the time expending energy, and there have been reports of polar bears swimming almost twice that far in seas cold enough to kill any animal, except the various marine species, within a few minutes.

This unparalleled resistance to cold is explained in part—and only in part—by the animal's unusual fur. Unless it has been temporarily stained by contact with some sort of mineral or organic matter, it usually varies in color from snow white or ivory to yellowish. (The latter hue, most common in summer, is thought to result from oxidation caused by the sun.) Appearing white because it reflects and scatters all visible rays of the spectrum, the coat is composed of clear, hollow hairs. Hollow guard hairs, an effective form of insulation, are common to deer and many other animals, but a polar bear's are different.

Several years ago, Canadian biologists found that aerial censusing of polar bears was difficult because the animals were often invisible against snow, and infrared photography—which normally reveals warm-blooded animals—mysteriously failed. The fur was giving off no heat, or at any rate insufficient heat for infrared detection. Ultraviolet photography subsequently solved the problem, because snow reflects most of the sun's ultraviolet radiation while the fur absorbs it, thereby creating a contrast on the film. The infrared failure intrigued Richard Grojean, an electrical and computer engineering professor whose investigations led to a new understanding of the way in which a polar bear's coat functions to keep it warm.

The hollow hairs trap ultraviolet radiation and conduct it to the bear's skin, which is as black as the animal's nose and lips. They catch light coming from any direction and, for reasons not

A female leads a cub about while waiting for pack ice to form on lower Hudson Bay. The ice will allow them to move out on the bay for the winter seal hunt. Some cubs remain with their mothers for as long as three years.

It is difficult to tell whether this bear is bellowing or merely yawning. Polar bears have a fairly wide range of vocalizations, but are not among the noisiest of species.

A male bear on the shore of Hudson Bay sits up and gazes intently at something that has caught its attention. It is not at all nervous about enemies—it has none except where hunted—but it is always on the alert for prey or carrion.

Pack ice has begun to form along the Manitoba shore, but does not yet reach far enough across the waters of Hudson Bay, and these bears are wandering restlessly. Sometimes they follow one another on treks that appear aimless to the human observer.

yet understood, the trapped ultraviolet energy flows only inward to the skin with almost no loss of heat. Grojean and his colleagues at Northeastern University in Boston found that the fur is ninety-five percent efficient in converting the ultraviolet rays into usable heat.

Although it seems obvious that the absorbed energy is important in maintaining body temperature even at forty degrees F below zero, the heat-conveyor guard hairs alone would not suffice (especially when immersed in water), nor would the woolly undercoat. Beneath the skin lies a thick layer of fat, comparable to the blubber of marine mammals. It may be four inches thick, or thicker when the animal has put on weight prior to denning, and like the guard hairs, it provides both insulation and buoyancy. Furthermore, the, circulatory system is unusual in that it includes a "countercurrent" blood system, which cools the blood as it flows toward the body surface and warms it on the return flow—"an automatic heat engine, like a seal's," as one researcher has described it.

At one time, polar bears were in such severe decline as to be threatened with extinction. They probably never have been as abundant as black bears are and brown bears were, and they were seriously depleted by a combination of almost uncontrolled trophy and skin hunting plus subsistence hunting by the Eskimo. In 1967, Canada, the United States, Denmark, Norway, and

A large male bear, with water streaming from his flanks and belly, patrols an expanse of ice floes in the upper Northwest Territories.

A polar bear is as much at home in the water as on an ice floe. These animals have been known to swim fifty to sixty miles without a rest at an average speed of five or six miles an hour.

A Manitoba polar bear paws for food during the warm season. Unlike other bears, polar bears lose weight in summer because reduced ice hampers seal hunting.

Russia agreed to a conservation treaty. Most of the polar bear populations are now totally protected, although Canada, which has always had relatively high numbers of them—possibly more than half of the world's total—allows Eskimo to hunt them under an annual quota system. The Inuit are permitted, in turn, to use a small percentage of the quota by guiding a limited number of trophy hunters.

Canada now has about fifteen thousand polar bears. Most of these live above the Arctic Circle, in the upper reaches of the Northwest Territories, but Canada also has the most southerly—and most inland—population, along the lower western edge of Hudson Bay. The world's total population is somewhere between twenty thousand and forty thousand (nearer the upper figure, according to some estimates) and is generally stable, even increasing in some areas. Distribution is circumpolar, with bears roaming the sea ice and coasts of Alaska, Canada, Greenland, Norway's Svalbard Islands, and the Soviet Union. Normally, they are found only as far south as the pack ice.

Both their wandering and their welfare depend in large measure on the abundance and move-

A bear wanders among willows in the Churchill area, looking for food. Until the temperature drops and sufficient ice forms, prey will be meager, so the bears now become less active and conserve energy.

A polar bear's huge tracks tend to be blurred and indistinct, not only because of shifting, blowing snow but because the soles of the feet are haired for traction and insulation.

Although individual tracks may he blurry, there is no mistaking a polar bear trail in crusted snow.

At Churchill, Manitoba, a polar bear stands on its hind legs and stretches to peer into a bunkhouse used by observers.

ments of seals—haired seals the year round and ring-seal pups taken from their ice dens in spring. When seals are plentiful, a bear usually will kill one every few days, and in order to maintain its body weight it needs a successful hunt every five or six days. It can, however, live off its fat reserves for weeks if no prey is caught. Then, when it makes a kill or finds some outsized feast, such as a dead walrus or whale, it can devour as much as 150 pounds, for its stomach is huge.

Early observers, noting extreme selectivity and apparent wastefulness in the polar bear's habit of consuming the blubber and some skin but leaving most or all of the meat for scavenging arctic foxes and birds, surmised that the species must kill so many seals and come upon so many other carcasses as to be constantly sated. This is not the case. The reason is that the blubber contains less protein than the flesh. If a bear were to ingest large quantities of protein in a severely cold climate, it would need to melt snow in its mouth because it would need large quantities of

This polar bear is peering from behind a snow drift. When stalking seals over ice rather than from the water, bears often keep hidden behind pressure ridges, making a circuitous approach so that the prey will not detect an enemy and slip into the water.

At Kane Basin in the arctic, a bear lopes along searching for a seal. The bear will also look for small holes in the ice. Seals swimming under the ice punch these holes and periodically come up for air.

water to get rid of nitrogen wastes.

Furthermore, this species, which is more strictly carnivorous than any other bear, does eat other prey and carrion, including fish, birds, crabs, rodents, eggs, hares, and even reindeer. In addition, it eats berries and other plants when it can find them, particularly in summer in the southernmost part of the range. Still, it loses weight in summer when the diet is most varied but least nutritious. In early autumn it subsists partially on its own stored fat as it awaits the thickening and expansion of ice that facilitates seal hunting.

The animal's highly evolved seal-hunting techniques are marvelous to behold. Since seals are considerably faster than a bear in the water, few of them are taken by pursuit or far from ice. The bear patrols the floes, the coast, and the edges of leads, searching for a seal resting on the ice. Its hearing is keen, its eyesight better than that of other bears,

A bear rises up and sniffs the wind. With its head in this position, it is not at the moment using its eyes for detection, but its remarkable sense of smell instead. The animal can smell a seal at great distances.

A polar bear leaps across open water from ice floe to ice floe. Much the same sort of leap is often used to capture seals, the polar bear's primary food. The bear stalks as close as possible, then makes a sudden rush or leaping pounce.

A bear swims gracefully underwater. If, before entering the water, it spotted a seal on the edge of a floe, it will come up close enough to the prey to heave out of the water and grab the seal's head or neck before it can move out of the way.

A polar bear of the Svalbard Islands stands over its kill. These bears were once thought to be savagely and inexplicably wasteful because they eat blubber and leave meat behind. Now it is understood that the bears practice prudent dietary habits: if they were to eat the protein-rich meat, they would need great quantities of fresh water to flush away nitrogen wastes.

and it will investigate any dark shape or spot it sees. Its sense of smell is incredible. It can easily detect a seal den covered by three feet of snow or ice, and observers have declared that it can smell a seal out of water twenty miles away. If such distances are an exaggeration (and they do invite skepticism), certainly the bear has some instinctive way of almost pinpointing the location of distant prey, hidden far beyond a series of drifts and ice heaves. When a seal is located dozing close to the brink of the ice, the bear approaches circuitously, slips into the water (or dives in splashily if far enough away to dispense with caution), swims toward its quarry silently, and suddenly heaves up onto the ice to grab the seal in its jaws and strike it with a paw.

Polar bears also have the ability to locate "plunge holes" in the ice, far from open water. Most of these are not large enough for a seal to use them comfortably when it wants to come out of the water or go back in. They are really breathing holes where a seal comes periodically to stick

Its coat powdered with snow on a cold November day in Manitoba, a bear dozes among the drifts in total comfort. Polar bears are so thoroughly adapted to an arctic existence that they are impervious to intense cold but easily become overheated in temperatures that are comfortable for more southerly species.

its head or just its nose up for air. The hole may sometimes be less than ten inches in diameter, not even half the diameter of an adult seal, and it may be partly frozen over. Still, the bear can find it and wait close to it, patient and motionless for hours, until a seal appears. Then the bear lunges, makes a killing snatch with its jaws, and pulls the prey up through the hole, sometimes stretching and literally dismantling the dead seal, whose body is far too large to come easily through the opening. The polar bear's neck is proportionally longer than the necks of its relatives, and the neck and shoulder muscles are exceptionally powerful—apparently adaptations to this hunting method. Another method is a low-bellied stalk toward a resting seal, using drifts and ridges for cover when possible and also paying attention to wind direction. A dozing seal awakens at least a couple of times per minute to raise its head and look around for danger. The seal positions itself close enough to water for a diving escape. The bear moves forward while the seal's head is down, but stops and remains motionless like a stalking cat when the head comes up. At last, when the distance is only a few yards, the bear charges with terrific speed.

The combination of instinct and intelligence in polar bears is uncanny. One researcher

Bears can often be observed dozing on ice. They can sleep comfortably in weather that would kill a human being.

This polar bear is rolling in snow to dry its fur. Very often they shake themselves like dogs, but in mild weather they sometimes just let the water stream off as they walk.

A mother polar bear communicates with her two cubs. Earlier in this century, the species was nearly on the brink of extinction, but now polar bear populations are thriving, stable, and even increasing in some parts of the world.

A bear prowls a frozen tundra pond in the forlorn hope of spotting prey. If this is a pregnant female or one with cubs, it will dig a winter den in or under a snow bank. Males do not den.

watched a bear spring a trap by pushing a large rock onto the trigger pan before eating the bait. This behavior has been observed in other bear species, but polar bears have additional abilities. They have been observed more than once covering their black noses with a paw while stalking a seal, thus rendering their white camouflage almost total. (In a rather hard-to-credit Eskimo version of this story, a chunk of snow or ice is held or rolled in front of the nose.) Even the most intelligent primates lack the self-awareness that humans possess—instantly recognizing others of their own kind, of course, but remaining unaware of their own appearance. As for the polar bear, it does not gaze with interest at its own reflection in the water and surely cannot know—consciously—that it has a big black nose in need of concealment. This behavioral quirk must be an evolved muscular or instinctive habit inherited from ancestors that happened to stalk with their feet moving ahead of their faces.

But more than inherited instinct would seem to be involved in the use of tools, a form of behavior seen in very few animals other than man. Polar bears have been observed using chunks of ice to hammer and break seal dens in order to get at the pups.

The bears' own denning sites are almost colonial in nature, like the thickly concentrated nesting colonies of seabirds. The sites are located in nearly a score of known locations and, it is thought, a few unknown locations. Under severe blizzard conditions, males dig temporary shelters in and under snow drifts but do not den in the true sense. Where food is scarce, their metabolism may slow somewhat, and there is evidence of metabolic shifts during lean summer periods as well, but males continue to be more or less nomadic all year. Likewise, females

that are not pregnant take shelter only under severe conditions. But pregnant females dig maternity dens in snow banks, mostly in October or early November but, surprisingly, a bit later in some regions. The timing may depend more on food availability than on weather or the total darkness of arctic winter.

Mention has been made of the southernmost population of polar bears, along the lower western edge of Hudson Bay in Manitoba. Here lies the little settlement of Churchill, at the mouth of a river of that name and just west of a point known as Cape Churchill. The town is Canada's northernmost deepwater port but is better known—in fact, world-renowned—as the "Polar Bear Capital of the World," a mecca for professional researchers as well as adventurous tourists. In spring, ice floes drift and are blown from the upper bay down to the southwestern shores, carrying great numbers of the bears, and the animals disperse inland during the summer, then begin a long return trek northward along the shore zone. In autumn, as many as a thousand bears may be in the vicinity of Churchill. This is the world's largest concentration, and some forty miles to the south is one of the world's largest denning areas, discovered in 1969 and now designated as a provincial park (covering over six thousand square miles!) to protect the bears.

These two massive and powerful animals may seem at first glance to be fighting, but they have not bared their teeth. They are merely playing roughly. Awaiting the formation of pack ice along the lower reaches of Hudson Bay, they will show such gregarious tendencies only until they can resume seal hunting.

Researchers taking measurements of animals in far-flung parts of the polar bear realm have recorded no animal whose size shatters previous records, but the size indicated by those records is impressive enough. A specimen collected long ago for the Carnegie Museum was weighed in pieces after it was shot. The total weight, despite the unavoidable loss of some body fluids, was 1,728 pounds. It was even larger than the biggest brown bear ever recorded, and another was larger still, with a recorded weight of 2,210 pounds.

A more typical mature male will weigh between eight hundred and eleven hundred pounds and will be about four feet high at the shoulder and eight feet long, which means that when it stands upright on its hind legs its head is apt to be ten feet or more above the ground. Females

are considerably smaller, seldom reaching a weight of seven hundred pounds. To a human observer who has not grown accustomed to weighing polar bears, that seems quite large enough. But in view of current conservation efforts and continuing field research, it seems likely that sooner or later the field biologists will come across a polar bear outweighing any yet recorded.

Even if no such record-breaker is ever encountered, the weights, measurements, and population censuses now being taken are gratifying. If precautions and restrictions can be continued and increased to prevent oil exploration and extraction from disrupting or polluting habitat, there is a promising future for the nomadic giants of the north that were once threatened with extinction.

These bears are sniffing each other's muzzle in initial greeting. Afterward they may silently go their separate ways or they may dance around, playfully biting and wrestling.

Young bears at Churchill, Manitoba, are often seen play fighting. All species of bears seem to enjoy mock fights, which undoubtedly help them learn how to defend themselves and assert dominance.

A procession of bears is clearly visible as shadows lengthen over a snow field. When the sun is high, however, these animals become almost invisible against their white background when someone tries to watch them from a distance.

Bears exhibit gregarious behavior during their Churchill sojourn. When they leave to resume seal hunting, all but the sows with cubs again become solitary.

Even when the sun is bright, a polar
bear does not always appear white.
The direction of illumination can
turn it into a dark, spectral silhouette
moving over streaked and dappled
patches of glare and shadow.

PHOTO CREDITS

INDEX BY PAGE

INDEX BY PHOTOGRAPHER